JAMESTOWN EDUCATION

TIMED READINGS
in Literature
BOOK TEN

Edward Spargo, Editor

Selections & Questions
for this Edition:
Henry Billings
Melissa Billings

Fifty 400-Word Passages
with Questions for
Building Reading Speed

Glencoe
McGraw-Hill

New York, New York   Columbus, Ohio   Chicago, Illinois   Peoria, Illinois   Woodland Hills, California

JAMESTOWN EDUCATION

Titles in This Series
Timed Readings, Third Edition
Timed Readings in Literature

Teaching Notes are available for this text and
will be sent to the instructor. Please write on
school stationery; tell us what grade
you teach and identify the text.

Glencoe/McGraw-Hill

A Division of The McGraw-Hill Companies

Send all inquiries to:
Glencoe/McGraw-Hill
8787 Orion Place
Columbus, OH 43240-4027

Cover and text design by Deborah Hulsey Christie

Printed in the United States of America

7 8 9 10 11 12 13 14 021 10 09 08 07 06 05 04

ISBN 0-89061-523-3

Contents

Introduction to the Student

These *Timed Readings in Literature* are designed to help you become a faster and better reader. As you progress through the book, you will find yourself growing in reading speed and comprehension. You will be challenged to increase your reading rate while maintaining a high level of comprehension.

Reading, like most things, improves with practice. If you practice improving your reading speed, you will improve. As you will see, the rewards of improved reading speed will be well worth your time and effort.

Why Read Faster?

The quick and simple answer is that faster readers are better readers. Does this statement surprise you? You might think that fast readers would miss something and their comprehension might suffer. This is not true, for two reasons:

1. Faster readers comprehend faster. When you read faster, the writer's message is coming to you faster and makes sense sooner. Ideas are interconnected. The writer's thoughts are all tied together, each one leading to the next. The more quickly you can see how ideas are related to each other, the more quickly you can comprehend the meaning of what you are reading.

2. Faster readers concentrate better. Concentration is essential for comprehension. If your mind is wandering you can't understand what you are reading. A lack of concentration causes you to re-read, sometimes over and over, in order to comprehend. Faster readers concentrate better because there's less time for distractions to interfere. Comprehension, in turn, contributes to concentration. If you are concentrating and comprehending, you will not become distracted.

Want to Read More?

Do you wish that you could read more? (or, at least, would you like to do your required reading in less time?) Faster reading will help.

The illustration on the next page shows the number of books someone might read over a period of ten years. Let's see what faster reading could

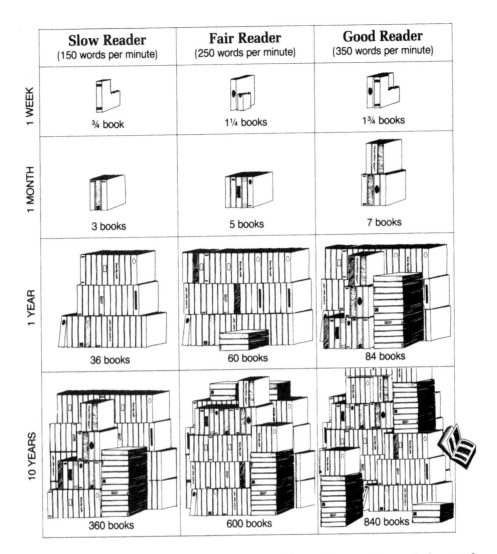

	Slow Reader (150 words per minute)	**Fair Reader** (250 words per minute)	**Good Reader** (350 words per minute)
1 WEEK	¾ book	1¼ books	1¾ books
1 MONTH	3 books	5 books	7 books
1 YEAR	36 books	60 books	84 books
10 YEARS	360 books	600 books	840 books

do for you. Look at the stack of books read by a slow reader and the stack read by a good reader. (We show a speed of 350 words a minute for our "good" reader, but many fast readers can more than double that speed.) Let's say, however, that you are now reading at a rate of 150 words a minute. The illustration shows you reading 36 books a year. By increasing your reading speed to 250 words a minute, you could increase the number of books to 60 a year.

We have arrived at these numbers by assuming that the readers in our illustration read for one hour a day, six days a week, and that an average book is about 72,000 words long. Many people do not read that much, but they might if they could learn to read better and faster.

Faster reading doesn't *take* time, it *saves* time!

Acquisitional *vs.* Recreational Reading

Timed Readings in Literature gives practice in a certain kind of reading: recreational reading. Recreational reading of novels and short stories is different from the kind of reading you must employ with textbooks. You read a textbook to *acquire* facts and information. That is acquisitional reading, reading that is careful and deliberate—you cannot afford to miss something you may be quizzed on later. Acquisitional reading speed must be slower than recreational reading speed.

The practice you will be doing in this book will help you develop a high reading speed suitable for literature.

Why Practice on Literature?

If acquisitional reading is so useful and important for students, why should you spend valuable class time learning to read literature faster? Shouldn't you be learning to read textbooks faster and better? Believe it or not, you are! That's right: the reading speed and skills you develop from this book will transfer to your textbooks and to other study reading. Here are some of the ways this happens.

1. The practice effect. In the dictionary, *practice* is defined as systematic exercise to gain proficiency. In other words, repeated drill brings improvement. You know from your own experience that when you practice anything—from piano to basketball—you become better at it. The same holds true for reading. As you are doing the drills and exercises in these books, you are practicing *all* of your reading skills at the same time. With practice you become a fluent reader and comprehender—a better reader of everything you read.

2. Using context. Good readers are aware of context and use it to aid understanding. Context refers to the words surrounding those you are reading. Meaning, you see, does not come from a single word, or even a single sentence—it is conveyed within the whole context of what you are reading.

The language of literature is rich with meaning. The storyteller is trying to *please* the reader, not *teach* the reader. The writer wants to share feelings and experiences with the reader, to reach him or her in a personal way. As you practice reading literature, you are developing your skill in using context to extract the full measure of meaning and appreciation. These same context skills can be put to work when you are reading textbooks to help you organize facts into a meaningful body of knowledge.

3. Vocabulary growth. Our early vocabulary comes from listening—to our families, friends, television, teachers, and classmates. We learn and understand new words as we hear them being used by others. In fact, the more times we encounter a word, the better we understand it. Finally, it becomes ours, part of our permanent vocabulary of words we know and use.

As time goes by, an increasing number of words is introduced to us through recreational reading. Most of the words we know come from reading—words we have never looked up in a dictionary, but whose meanings have become clear to us through seeing them again and again until they are finally ours. Literature, the kind you will be reading in this book, provides countless opportunities for meeting and learning new words. Literature, as you have seen, also provides the context for seeing these new words used with precision and effect. As you work through the pages in this book, you will be developing a larger and stronger vocabulary—a storehouse of words that become your tools for learning.

4. Skills transfer. You are using this book to develop your ability to read literature with increased speed and comprehension. With regular practice and a little effort, you will be successful in reaching that goal.

As we mentioned, you will also be improving your context skills and building a bigger vocabulary. These are all wonderful results from using this book.

But, perhaps the greatest benefit of all is the application of these improvements to all of your reading tasks, not just literature. Using this book will make you a better reader, and *better readers read everything better.*

Reading Literature Faster

Through literature we share an experience with a writer. That experience may be presented as a conversation, a character or scene, an emotion, or an event.

Let's examine these four kinds of presentation. Let's see if there are characteristics or clues we can use to help us identify each kind. Once we know what we are expected to experience, we can read more intelligently and more quickly.

When you are working in this book, your instructor will schedule a few moments for you to preview each selection before timing begins. Use the preview time to scan the selection rapidly, looking for one of the following kinds of presentation.

1. Reading and Understanding a Conversation

A conversation is intended to tell us what characters are thinking or feeling—the best way to do this is through their own words.

Read the following conversation between George and his mother, an excerpt from "George's Mother" by Stephen Crane:

> Finally he said savagely: "Damn these early hours!" His mother jumped as if he had thrown a missile at her. "Why, George—" she began.
>
> George broke in again. "Oh, I know all that—but this gettin' up in th' mornin' so early just makes me sick. Jest when a man is gettin' his mornin' nap he's gotta get up. I—"
>
> "George, dear," said his mother, "yeh know I hate yeh to swear, dear. Now, please don't." She looked beseechingly at him.
>
> He made a swift gesture. "Well, I ain't swearin', am I?" he demanded. "I was only sayin' that this gettin'-up business gives me a pain, wasn't I?"
>
> "Well, yeh know how swearin' hurts me," protested the little old woman. She seemed about to sob. She gazed off . . . apparently recalling persons who had never been profane.

First, is this a conversation? Yes, we know it is. There are quotation marks throughout indicating words spoken by the characters. So, to identify a conversation, we look for quotation marks.

Next, does this conversation tell us what the characters are thinking or feeling? It certainly does—this conversation is unmistakably clear. We know how George *feels* about getting up in the morning, and we know how his mother *feels* about profanity.

Finally, how should we read this and other conversations we encounter in literature? Join the conversation; pretend you are one of the speakers and that these are your own words. Listen to the other character as though words are being addressed to you.

Conversations can be read quickly and understood well when you recognize them and become part of them.

2. Reading About and Understanding a Character or Scene

How do we learn about a character? There are many ways. Writers introduce characters (1) by telling us what they look like; (2) by what they say; (3) by the things they do; and (4) by telling us what others think and say about them:

> He was a staid, placid gentleman, something past the prime of life, yet upright in his carriage for all that, and slim as a greyhound. He was well mounted upon a sturdy chestnut cob, and had the graceful seat of an experienced horseman; while his riding gear, though free from such fopperies as were then in vogue, was handsome and well chosen. He wore a riding coat of a somewhat brighter green than might have been expected to suit the taste of a gentleman of his years, with a short, black velvet cape, and laced pocket holes and cuffs, all of a jaunty fashion; his linen too, was of the finest kind, worked in a rich pattern at the wrists and throat, and scrupulously white. Although he seemed, judging from the mud he had picked up on the way, to have come from London, his horse was as smooth and cool as his own iron-gray periwig and pigtail.

Obviously a character is being introduced to us in this passage from *Barnaby Rudge* by Charles Dickens. We are told how he carries himself and how he is dressed. We even know a little about what he has been doing.

The question to ask yourself is: Is this character lifelike and real? Real characters should be like real people—good and bad, happy and sad, alike and different. In reading about characters, look for the same details you look for in all people.

Similarly, when a scene or location is being described, look for words which tell about size, shape, color, appearance. Such descriptor words help us picture in our minds the place being described. Try to visualize the scene as you read.

3. Experiencing an Emotion Through Literature

When a writer presents an emotion for us to experience, the intent is to produce an effect within us. The intended effect may be pity, fear, revulsion, or some other emotion. The writer wants us to *feel* something.

In the following passage from *Jane Eyre* by Charlotte Brontë, what emotions are we expected to feel for the character?

> John had not much affection for his mother and sisters, and an antipathy to me. He bullied and punished me; not two or three times in the week, not once or twice in the day, but continually: every nerve I had feared him, and every morsel of flesh on my bones shrank when he came near. There were moments when I was bewildered by the terror he inspired, because I had no appeal whatever against either his menaces or his inflictions; the servants did not like to offend their young master by taking my part against him, and Mrs. Reed was blind and deaf on the subject: She never saw him strike or heard him abuse me, though he did both now and then in her very presence; more frequently behind her back.

Do you feel sorry for this girl because she is being abused? Do you feel compassion because she is suffering? Are you suffering with her? Do you feel anger toward her abuser? What other effects are intended? How are these effects produced?

Emotional and provocative words and expressions have been employed by the writer to paint a vivid portrait of her character's predicament. Can you identify some of the words? What did John do? He *bullied, struck, punished,* and *abused.* The girl felt fear, bewilderment, and terror. These very expressive and emotional words and phrases are the clues provided by the writer to help her readers read and comprehend effectively.

4. Reading About and Understanding an Event

In describing an event—a series of actions—the writer is telling us a story, and the elements of the story are presented in some kind of order or pattern. Read this passage from *Around the World in Eighty Days* by Jules Verne:

> Mr. Fogg and his two companions took their places on a bench opposite the desks of the magistrate and his clerk. Immediately after, Judge Obadiah, a fat, round man, followed by the clerk, entered. He proceeded to take down a wig which was hanging on a nail, and put it hurriedly on his head.
>
> "The first case," said he. Then, putting his hand to his head, he exclaimed "Heh! This is not my wig!"
>
> "No, your worship," returned the clerk, "it is mine."
>
> "My dear Mr. Oysterpuff, how can a judge give a wise sentence in a clerk's wig?"
>
> The wigs were exchanged.

Did you see how this little story was told? The events in the story were presented in chronological order—from first to last as they occurred. This is a frequently used and easily recognized pattern, but not the only one writers use. The story could have been told in reverse—the story could have opened with the judge wearing the wrong wig and then gone on to explain how the mistake happened.

In passages like these, look for the events in the story and see how they are related, how one event follows or builds on the other. By recognizing the pattern of storytelling and using the pattern as an aid to organizing and understanding the events, you can become a better and faster reader.

How to Use This Book

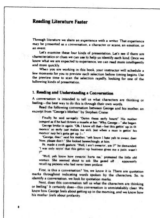

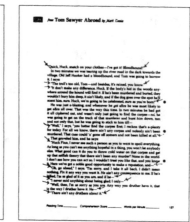

1 Read the lessons
First, read the lessons on pages 8 through 11. These lessons teach you how to recognize and identify the kinds of presentation you encounter in literature and in the selections in this book.

2 Preview
Find a literature selection to read and wait for your instructor's signal to preview. You will have 30 seconds to preview (scan) the selection to identify the author's kind of presentation.

3 Begin reading
When your instructor gives you the signal, begin reading. Read at a slightly faster-than-normal speed. Read well enough so that you will be able to answer questions about what you have read.

7 Fill in the progress graph
Enter your score and plot your reading time on the graph on page 118 or 119. The right-hand side of the graph shows your words-per-minute reading speed. Write this number at the bottom of the page on the line labeled *Words per Minute.*

4 Record your time

When you finish reading, look at the black-board and note your reading time. Your reading time will be the lowest time remaining on the board, or the next number to be erased. Write this time at the bottom of the page on the line labeled *Reading Time.*

5 Answer the questions

Answer the ten questions on the next page. There are five fact questions and five thought questions. Pick the *best* answer to each question and put an x in the box beside it.

6 Correct your answers

Using the Answer Key on pages 116 and 117, correct your work. Circle your wrong answers and put an x in the box you should have marked. Score 10 points for each correct answer. Write your score at the bottom of the page on the line labeled *Comprehension Score.*

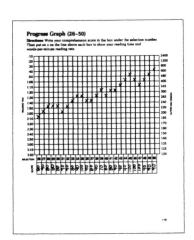

Instructions for the Pacing Drills

From time to time your instructor may wish to conduct pacing drills using *Timed Readings*. For this work you need to use the Pacing Dots printed in the margins of your book pages. The dots will help you regulate your reading speed to match the pace set by your instructor or announced on the reading cassette tape.

Pacing Dots

You will be reading at the correct pace if you are at the dot when your instructor says "Mark" or when you hear a tone on the tape. If you are ahead of the pace, read a little more slowly; if you are behind the pace, increase your reading speed. Try to match the pace exactly.

Follow these steps.

Step 1: Record the pace. At the bottom of the page, write on the line labeled *Words per Minute* the rate announced by the instructor or by the speaker on the tape.

Step 2: Begin reading. Wait for the signal to begin reading. Read at a slightly faster-than-normal speed. You will not know how on-target your pace is until you hear your instructor say "Mark" or until you hear the first tone on the tape. After a little practice you will be able to select an appropriate starting speed most of the time.

Step 3: Adjust your pace. As you read, try to match the pace set by the instructor or the tape. Read more slowly or more quickly as necessary. You should be reading the line beside the dot when you hear the pacing signal. The pacing sounds may distract you at first. Don't worry about it. Keep reading and your concentration will return.

Step 4: Stop and answer questions. Stop reading when you are told to, even if you have not finished the selection. Answer the questions right away. Correct your work and record your score on the line *Comprehension Score*. Strive to maintain 80 percent comprehension on each drill as you gradually increase your pace.

Step 5: Fill in the pacing graph. Transfer your words-per-minute rate to the box labeled *Pace* on the pacing graph on page 120. Then plot your comprehension score on the line above the box.

These pacing drills are designed to help you become a more flexible reader. They encourage you to "break out" of a pattern of reading everything at the same speed.

The drills help in other ways, too. Sometimes in a reading program you reach a certain level and bog down. You don't seem able to move on and progress. The pacing drills will help you to work your way out of such slumps and get your reading program moving again.

Mr. Collins was not a sensible man, and the deficiency of nature had been but little assisted by education or society, the greatest part of his life having been spent under the guidance of an illiterate and miserly father; and though he belonged to one of the universities, he had merely kept the necessary terms, without forming at it any useful acquaintance. The subjection in which his father had brought him up had given him originally great humility of manner; but it was now a good deal counteracted by the self-conceit of a weak head, living in retirement, and the consequential feelings of early and unexpected prosperity. A fortunate chance had recommended him to Lady Catherine de Bourgh when the living of Hunsford was vacant, and the respect which he felt for her high rank and his veneration for her as his patroness, mingling with a very good opinion of himself, of his authority as a clergyman, and his right as a rector, made him altogether a mixture of pride and obsequiousness, self-importance and humility.

Having now a good house and a very sufficient income, he intended to marry; and in seeking a reconciliation with the Longbourn family he had a wife in view, as he meant to choose one of the daughters, if he found them as handsome and amiable as they were represented by common report. This was his plan of amends—of atonement—for inheriting their father's estate; and he thought it an excellent one, full of eligibility and suitableness, and excessively generous and disinterested on his own part.

His plan did not vary on seeing them. Miss Bennet's lovely face confirmed his views, and he established all his strictest notions of what was due to seniority; and for the first evening she was his settled choice. The next morning, however, made an alteration; for in a quarter of an hour's tete-a-tete with Mrs. Bennet before breakfast, a conversation beginning with his parsonage house, and leading naturally to the avowal of his hopes that a mistress for it might be found at Longbourn, produced from her, amid very complaisant smiles and general encouragement, a caution against the very Jane he had fixed on. "As to her younger daughter, she could not take upon her to say—her eldest daughter she must just mention—she felt it incumbent on her to hint, was likely to be very soon engaged."

Recalling Facts

1. Mr. Collins was
   - ☐ a. an intellectual.
   - ☐ b. not very reasonable.
   - ☐ c. a man of great common sense.

2. Mr. Collins had become
   - ☐ a. conceited.
   - ☐ b. poverty stricken.
   - ☐ c. a miser.

3. Mr. Collins was a
   - ☐ a. university president.
   - ☐ b. lawyer.
   - ☐ c. clergyman.

4. Mr. Collins sought
   - ☐ a. reconciliation with the Longbourn family.
   - ☐ b. to remain a bachelor.
   - ☐ c. to leave his fortune to charity.

5. The eldest Miss Bennet was likely to be
   - ☐ a. sent off to school.
   - ☐ b. rejected because of her appearance.
   - ☐ c. engaged in the near future.

Understanding the Passage

6. Mr. Collins's father
   - ☐ a. did little to guide his son.
   - ☐ b. provided his son with no money.
   - ☐ c. arranged for his son's marriage.

7. Mr. Collins's personality changed somewhat when he
   - ☐ a. fell in love.
   - ☐ b. met Miss Bennet.
   - ☐ c. became wealthy.

8. Mr. Collins felt he should marry
   - ☐ a. a widow.
   - ☐ b. one of Mrs. Bennet's daughters.
   - ☐ c. Lady Catherine.

9. Mr. Collins
   - ☐ a. knew the Longbourn family well.
   - ☐ b. had never met the daughters before.
   - ☐ c. wanted to marry for love.

10. Mr. Collins thought he should marry Mrs. Bennet's
    - ☐ a. prettiest daughter.
    - ☐ b. oldest daughter.
    - ☐ c. youngest daughter.

from **The Disabled Soldier** *by Oliver Goldsmith*

No observation is more common, and at the same time more true, than that one half of the world are ignorant how the other half lives. The misfortunes of the great are held up to engage our attentions; are enlarged upon in tones of declamation; and the world is called upon to gaze at the noble sufferers: the great, under the pressure of calamity, are conscious of several others sympathizing with their distress; and have, at once, the comfort of admiration and pity.

There is nothing magnanimous in bearing misfortunes with fortitude when the whole world is looking on: men in such circumstances will act bravely even from motives of vanity: but he who, in the vale of obscurity, can brave adversity; who without friends to encourage, acquaintances to pity, or even without hope to alleviate his misfortunes, can behave with tranquility and indifference, is truly great: whether peasant or courtier, he deserves admiration, and should be held up for our imitation and respect.

While the slightest inconveniences of the great are magnified into calamities; while tragedy mouths out their suffering in all the strains of eloquence, the miseries of the poor are entirely disregarded; and yet some of the lower ranks of people undergo more real hardship in one day, than those of more exalted station suffer in their whole lives. It is inconceivable what difficulties the meanest of our common sailors and soldiers endure without regret; without passionately declaiming against providence, or calling their fellows to be gazers on their intrepidity. Every day is to them a day of misery, and yet they entertain their hard fate without repining.

With what indignation do I hear an Ovid, a Cicero, or a Rabutin complain of their misfortunes and hardships, whose greatest calamity was that of being unable to visit a certain spot on earth, to which they had foolishly attached an idea of happiness. Their distresses were pleasures, compared to what many of the adventuring poor every day endure without murmuring. They ate, drank, and slept; they had slaves to attend them, and were sure of subsistence for life; while many of their fellow creatures are obliged to wander without a friend to comfort them, and even without shelter from the severity of the season. I have been led into these reflections from accidentally meeting a poor fellow whom I knew when a boy.

Recalling Facts

1. When the great suffer
   they have
   □ a. sympathy.
   □ b. more pain.
   □ c. marvelous forebearance.

2. The truly great can withstand
   adversity with
   □ a. help from friends.
   □ b. indifference.
   □ c. hope for the future.

3. The miseries of the poor
   are entirely
   □ a. magnified.
   □ b. overrated.
   □ c. disregarded.

4. Great difficulties are endured
   without regret by
   □ a. farmers and fishermen.
   □ b. sailors and soldiers.
   □ c. courtiers and nobles.

5. The narrator began his
   reflections after meeting
   □ a. Rabutin.
   □ b. a stranger.
   □ c. a poor fellow.

Understanding the Passage

6. According to the narrator,
   the great
   □ a. know little about real
        suffering.
   □ b. hurt just as much as
        the poor.
   □ c. never have any reason
        to grieve.

7. The hardest thing to do
   is to suffer
   □ a. in the public eye.
   □ b. without friends.
   □ c. both a and b.

8. The narrator has no respect
   for people who
   □ a. suffer calamities.
   □ b. write about the
        hardships of others.
   □ c. complain about their
        misfortunes.

9. Ovid could not
   □ a. write very well.
   □ b. travel to a desired place
   □ c. both a and b.

10. The narrator is about to
    discuss the poor fellow with
    □ a. great sympathy.
    □ b. an air of distress.
    □ c. extreme disgust.

from **The Countess of Rudolstadt** *by George Sand*

Below the prison cells, a great smoky room, the heavy and dusky ceiling of which never received any other light than that of the fire kindled in a vast chimney place always filled with iron kettles hissing and grumbling in every tone, enclosed during the whole day the Schwartz family and their skillful culinary operations. While the wife mathematically combined the greatest possible number of dinners with the fewest imaginable provisions and ingredients, the husband, seated before a table black with ink and oil, by the light of a lamp always burning in that gloomy sanctuary, artistically composed the most formidable bills filled with the most fabulous details. The meagre dinners were for the goodly number of prisoners whom the officious keeper had succeeded in placing upon his list of boarders; the bills were to be presented to their bankers or relations, always without being submitted to the inspection of those who consumed this expensive nourishment. While the speculating couple earnestly gave themselves to their labor, two more peaceful personages, ensconced under the mantelpiece, lived there in silence, perfect strangers to the delights and profits of the operation. The first was a great lean cat, yellow, marked with burns, whose existence was passed in licking his paws and rolling in the ashes. The second was a young man, or rather a child, still more ugly in his kind, whose motionless and contemplative life was divided between the reading of an old worm-eaten folio, and eternal reveries which rather resembled the beatitude of an idiot than the meditation of a thinking being. The cat had been baptized by the child with the name of Beelzebub, doubtless by antithesis to that which the child had himself received from Mr. and Mrs. Schwartz, his father and mother: the pious and sacred name of Gottlieb.

Gottlieb, intended for an ecclesiastic, had, until fifteen years old, made good progress in his studies in the Protestant liturgy. But for the past four years he had lived inert and ill by the side of the fire, without wishing to walk, without desiring to see the sun, without the power of continuing his education. A rapid and disordered growth had reduced him to this state of languor and indolence. His long, thin legs could hardly support his immoderately tall and almost dislocated form. His arms were so weak and his hands so awkward that he touched nothing without breaking it.

Recalling Facts

1. The Schwartz family lived
   - □ a. in a prison cell.
   - □ b. below the prison cells.
   - □ c. next door to the prison.

2. Mr. Schwartz was in charge of
   - □ a. buying provisions.
   - □ b. cooking meals.
   - □ c. composing bills.

3. Beelzebub the cat had
   - □ a. many burns on his body.
   - □ b. one crippled paw.
   - □ c. a mean and calculating look.

4. Mr. and Mrs. Schwartz originally wanted Gottlieb to become
   - □ a. a prison warden.
   - □ b. a master chef.
   - □ c. an ecclesiastic.

5. For the past four years, Gottlieb had
   - □ a. worked hard to finish his education.
   - □ b. been in and out of prison.
   - □ c. suffered from a degenerative disease.

Understanding the Passage

6. Mr. and Mrs. Schwartz could best be described as
   - □ a. shrewd business people.
   - □ b. compassionate neighbors
   - □ c. heartless murderers.

7. The atmosphere in the Schwartz living quarters was
   - □ a. bright and cheerful.
   - □ b. dark and gloomy.
   - □ c. sad and inconsolable.

8. The bills sent to prisoners' bankers and relatives
   - □ a. exaggerated the true cost of the meals.
   - □ b. faithfully reflected the true cost of the meals.
   - □ c. underestimated the true cost of the meals.

9. Gottlieb could best be described as
   - □ a. pitiful.
   - □ b. ambitious.
   - □ c. frivolous.

10. Gottlieb was
    - □ a. oblivious to his parents' business dealings.
    - □ b. loved by all the prisoners.
    - □ c. eager to take over his parents' business.

from The Decline and Fall of the Roman Empire *by Edward Gibbon*

As the reign of Diocletian was more illustrious than that of any of his predecessors, so was his birth more abject and obscure. The strong claims of merit and of violence had frequently superseded the ideal prerogatives of nobility, but a distinct line of separation was hitherto preserved between the free and the servile part of mankind. The parents of Diocletian had been slaves in the house of Anulinus, a Roman senator; nor was he himself distinguished by any other name than that which he derived from a small town in Dalmatia, from whence his mother deduced her origin. It is, however, probable that his father obtained the freedom of the family, and that he soon acquired an office of scribe, which was commonly exercised by persons of his condition. Favorable oracles, or rather the consciousness of superior merit, prompted his aspiring son to pursue the profession of arms and the hopes of fortune; and it would be extremely curious to observe the graduation of arts and accidents which enabled him in the end to fulfill those oracles, and to display that merit to the world.

Diocletian was successively promoted to the government of Maesia, the honors of the consulship, and the important command of the guards of the palace. He distinguished his abilities in the Persian war; and after the death of Numerian, the slave, by the confession and judgment of his rivals, was declared the most worthy of the Imperial throne. The malice of religious zeal, whilst it arraigns the savage fierceness of his colleague Maximian, has affected to cast suspicion on the personal courage of the emperor Diocletian. It would not be easy to persuade us of the cowardice of a soldier of fortune who acquired and preserved the esteem of the legions, as well as the favor of so many warlike princes. Yet even calumny is sagacious enough to discover and to attack the most vulnerable part. The valor of Diocletian was never found inadequate to his duty, or to the occasion; but he appears not to have possessed the daring and generous spirit of a hero, who courts danger and fame, disdains artifice, and boldly challenges the allegiance of his equals. His abilities were useful rather than splendid—a vigorous mind improved by the experience and study of mankind; dexterity and application in business; and a judicious mixture of liberality and economy, of mildness and rigor.

Recalling Facts

1. The parents of Diocletian were
   □ a. nobles.
   □ b. merchants.
   □ c. slaves.

2. Diocletian was promoted to the government of
   □ a. Maesia.
   □ b. Dalmatia.
   □ c. Anulinus.

3. Diocletian won fame in the
   □ a. Greek war.
   □ b. Persian war.
   □ c. conquest of Gaul.

4. Diocletian became emperor after the death of
   □ a. Numerian.
   □ b. Maximian.
   □ c. Minimian.

5. Diocletian did not display the marks of
   □ a. an emperor.
   □ b. a hero.
   □ c. a businessman.

Understanding the Passage

6. In this society, social advancement was based on
   □ a. noble birth.
   □ b. merit and violence.
   □ c. either a or b.

7. The fastest route to the top for someone of low birth was
   □ a. the military.
   □ b. the clergy.
   □ c. politics.

8. Diocletian's personal courage
   □ a. was questioned by the narrator.
   □ b. waned after his war years.
   □ c. ranked with other great heroes.

9. As a soldier, Diocletian was
   □ a. despised by his rivals.
   □ b. generally well liked and respected.
   □ c. a foolhardy and careless commander.

10. Diocletian did not
   □ a. have many ambitions.
   □ b. have an ability to think clearly.
   □ c. seek out danger and notoriety.

Mrs. Archer, who had long been a widow, lived with her son, Newland, and her daughter, Janey, on West Twenty-eighth Street. An upper floor was dedicated to Newland, and the two women squeezed themselves into narrower quarters below. In an unclouded harmony of tastes and interests they cultivated ferns in Wardian cases, made macrame lace and wool embroidery on linen, collected American Revolutionary glazed ware, subscribed to "Good Words," and read Ouida's novels for the sake of the Italian atmosphere. (They preferred those about peasant life, because of the descriptions of scenery and the pleasanter sentiments, though in general they liked novels about people in society, whose motives and habits were more comprehensible; spoke severely of Dickens, who "had never drawn a gentleman"; and considered Thackeray less at home in the great world than Bulwer—who, however, was beginning to be thought old-fashioned.)

Mrs. and Miss Archer were both great lovers of scenery. It was what they principally sought and admired on their occasional travels abroad; considering architecture and painting as subjects for men, and chiefly for learned persons who read Ruskin. Mrs. Archer had been born a Newland, and mother and daughter, who were as like as sisters, were both, as people said, "true Newlands;" tall, pale, and slightly round shouldered, with long noses, sweet smiles and a kind of drooping distinction like that in certain faded Reynolds portraits. Their physical resemblance would have been complete if an elderly *embonpoint* had not stretched Mrs. Archer's black brocade, while Miss Archer's brown and purple poplins hung, as the years went on, more and more slackly on her virgin frame.

Mentally, the likeness between them, as Newland was aware, was less complete than their identical mannerisms often made it appear. The long habit of living together in mutually dependent intimacy had given them the same vocabulary, and the same habit of beginning their phrases "Mother thinks" or "Janey thinks," according as one or the other wished to advance an opinion of her own; but in reality, while Mrs. Archer's serene unimaginativeness rested easily in the accepted and familiar, Janey was subject to starts and aberrations of fancy welling up from springs of suppressed romance.

Mother and daughter adored each other and revered their son and brother; and Newland loved them with a tenderness made compunctious and uncritical by the sense of their exaggerated admiration, and by his secret satisfaction in it.

Recalling Facts

1. The top floor of Mrs. Archer's home was used by
   - ☐ a. Mrs. Archer herself.
   - ☐ b. Mrs. Archer's daughter.
   - ☐ c. Mrs. Archer's son.

2. Mrs. Archer liked to read novels by
   - ☐ a. Ruskin.
   - ☐ b. Ouida.
   - ☐ c. Dickens.

3. Mrs. and Miss Archer shared the same
   - ☐ a. living quarters.
   - ☐ b. mannerisms.
   - ☐ c. both a and b.

4. When Mrs. and Miss Archer traveled, they were chiefly interested in
   - ☐ a. beautiful scenery.
   - ☐ b. classic architecture.
   - ☐ c. art museums.

5. Janey Archer
   - ☐ a. loved her mother very much.
   - ☐ b. resented her mother's presence.
   - ☐ c. longed for a separate life.

Understanding the Passage

6. Mrs. and Miss Archer were
   - ☐ a. not as alike mentally as they were physically.
   - ☐ b. angry that they rarely saw Newland.
   - ☐ c. too busy to find time for their real interests.

7. Mrs. and Miss Archer seemed to
   - ☐ a. prefer looking on the bright side of life.
   - ☐ b. enjoy exploring the cities of Italian authors.
   - ☐ c. like reading about life in the slums of London.

8. Newland enjoyed
   - ☐ a. spending a lot of time alone
   - ☐ b. all the attention from his mother and sister.
   - ☐ c. studying architecture and painting.

9. Apparently, Miss Archer had
   - ☐ a. lived alone for a long time.
   - ☐ b. hidden desires for romance.
   - ☐ c. always harbored an unspoken resentment against Newland.

10. Mrs. and Miss Archer
    - ☐ a. depended on each other a great deal.
    - ☐ b. rarely left their living quarters.
    - ☐ c. bickered constantly but harmlessly.

When Ivan Ilyitch had graduated from the law school with the tenth rank, and received from his father some money for his uniform, he ordered a suit of Scharmer, added to his trinkets the little medal with the legend *respice finem*, bade the prince and principal farewell, ate a dinner with his schoolmates at Donon's, and furnished with a new and stylish trunk, linen, uniform, razors, and toilet articles, and a plaid, ordered or bought at the very best shops, he departed for the province, through his father's recommendation, in the capacity of government official, with a special message to the governor.

In the province, Ivan Ilyitch at once got himself into the same sort of easy and agreeable position as his position in the law school had been. He attended to his duties, pressed forward in his career, and at the same time enjoyed life in a cheerful and circumspect manner. From time to time, delegated by his chiefs, he visited the districts, bore himself with dignity toward both his superiors and subordinates, and, without overweening conceit, fulfilled with punctuality and incorruptible integrity the duties imposed upon him, preeminently in the affair of the dissenters.

Notwithstanding his youth, and his tendency to be gay and easygoing, he was, in matters of state, thoroughly discreet, and carried his official reserve even to sternness. but in society he was often merry and witty, and always good-natured, polite, and *bon enfant*, as he was called by his chief and his chief's wife, at whose house he was intimate.

While he was in the province, he had maintained relations with one of those ladies who are ready to fling themselves into the arms of an elegant young lawyer. There was also a dressmaker; and there were occasional sprees with visiting military assistants, and visits to some out-of-the-way street after supper: but all dissipation of this sort was attended with such a high tone, that it could not be qualified by hard names.

All was done with clean hands, with clean linen, with French words, and, above all, in company with the very highest society, and therefore with the approbation of those high in rank.

In this way, Ivan Ilyitch served five years, and a change was instituted in the service. The new tribunals were established: new men were needed.

And Ivan Ilyitch was chosen as one of the new men.

Ivan Ilyitch was offered the position of examining magistrate.

Recalling Facts

1. Ivan used the money his
   father gave him to buy
   □ a. his uniform.
   □ b. presents for his friends.
   □ c. some law books.

2. Ivan had dinner at Donon's
   with his
   □ a. father.
   □ b. principal.
   □ c. schoolmates.

3. When Ivan left for the
   province, he carried a
   message to
   □ a. government officials.
   □ b. the governor.
   □ c. his father.

4. One of Ivan's tasks was to
   deal with the
   □ a. revolutionaries.
   □ b. unruly servants.
   □ c. dissenters.

5. Ivan was promoted to
   examining magistrate after
   □ a. three years.
   □ b. five years.
   □ c. seven years.

Understanding the Passage

6. Apparently, Ivan's position in
   the province required
   □ a. impressive clothes.
   □ b. a medical degree.
   □ c. experience with the poor.

7. Ivan's position in the
   province
   □ a. did not prevent him
        from enjoying himself.
   □ b. demanded all his time
        and attention.
   □ c. did not suit his
        temperament.

8. Ivan's conduct on the job
   could best be described as
   □ a. lighthearted and
        unassuming.
   □ b. highly inflexible and
        autocratic.
   □ c. professional and
        dignified.

9. During his time off, Ivan
   □ a. maintained his stern
        manner.
   □ b. was outgoing and
        charming.
   □ c. usually stayed home
        and studied.

10. Ivan's flirtations with
    the ladies were
    □ a. always very polished
         and refined.
    □ b. frowned upon by his
         superiors.
    □ c. detrimental to Ivan's
         professional development

When Mr. Pontellier learned of his wife's intention to abandon their home and take up her residence elsewhere, he immediately wrote her a letter of unqualified disapproval and remonstrance. She had given reasons which he was unwilling to acknowledge as adequate. He hoped she had not acted upon her rash impulse, and he begged her to consider first, foremost, and above all else, what people would say. He was not dreaming of scandal when he uttered this warning; that was a thing which would never had entered into his mind to consider in connection with his wife's name or his own. He was simply thinking of his financial integrity. When people learned that Mrs. Edna Pontellier was moving into a smaller house, it might get noised about that the Pontelliers had met with reverses, and were forced to conduct their daily lives on a humbler scale than heretofore. It might do incalculable mischief to his business prospects.

But remembering Edna's whimsical turn of mind of late, and foreseeing that she had immediately acted upon her impetuous determination, he grasped the situation with his usual promptness, and handled it with his well-known business tact and cleverness.

The same mail which brought to Edna his letter of disapproval carried instructions—the most minute instructions—to a well-known architect concerning the remodeling of his home, changes which he had long contemplated, and which he desired carried forward during his temporary absence.

Expert and reliable packers and movers were engaged to convey the furniture, carpets, pictures, tableware—everything movable, in short—to places of security. And in an incredibly short time the Pontellier house was turned over to the artisans. There was to be an addition—a small snuggery; there was to be frescoing, and hardwood flooring was to be put into such rooms as had not yet been subjected to this improvement. Furthermore, in one of the daily papers appeared a brief notice to the effect that Mr. and Mrs. Pontellier were contemplating a summer sojourn abroad, and that their handsome residence on Esplanade Street was undergoing sumptous alterations, and would not be ready for occupancy until their return. Mr. Pontellier had saved appearances!

Edna admired the skill of his maneuver, and avoided any occasion to balk his intentions. When the situation as set forth by Mr. Pontellier was accepted and taken for granted, she was apparently satisfied that it should be so.

Recalling Facts

1. Mrs. Pontellier planned to
   □ a. remodel her bedroom.
   □ b. move out of her home.
   □ c. take over her husband's business.

2. Mr. Pontellier expressed his disapproval to Edna
   □ a. in a letter.
   □ b. through the newspaper.
   □ c. whenever they met.

3. Mr. Pontellier asked an architect to
   □ a. design a new house for his wife.
   □ b. remodel the Pontellier house.
   □ c. appraise the value of his home.

4. The artisans were instructed to
   □ a. put in hardwood floors.
   □ b. build a greenhouse.
   □ c. tear down all interior walls.

5. The Pontelliers' summer plans were announced
   □ a. at one of Mr. Pontellier's business meetings.
   □ b. in a local newspaper.
   □ c. from the pulpit of the local church.

Understanding the Passage

6. Mr. Pontellier did not want his wife to
   □ a. write him letters.
   □ b. take up a new residence.
   □ c. spend any money.

7. Mr. Pontellier's top priority was
   □ a. pleasing his wife.
   □ b. protecting his finances.
   □ c. continuing his philanthropy.

8. Mrs. Pontellier
   □ a. did not object to her husband's actions.
   □ b. decided to sue Mr. Pontellier for a divorce
   □ c. refused to let Mr. Pontellier remodel the house.

9. The Pontelliers apparently had
   □ a. very few friends.
   □ b. many large debts.
   □ c. a substantial amount of money.

10. Mr. Pontellier knew how to
    □ a. prevent ugly rumors from getting started.
    □ b. pack furniture for moving.
    □ c. change his wife's mind

Coppo Di Borghese Domenichi, who was of our city, and a man of reverence and authority in his day, and from his virtues and manners, much
more than from the nobility of his descent, worthy of everlasting remembrance, being now advanced in years, often took pleasure in the narration
of past events, to which his retentive memory and pleasing delivery lent
an unusual attraction. Among other interesting events he narrated to us
that there once lived in Florence a youth called Federigo, son of Messer
Philippo Alberighi, who for feats of arms and accomplishments was held
in higher esteem than any cavalier of his age in Tuscany. This young man ●
became deeply enamored of a lady called Monna Giovanna, reputed in
her time one of the most beautiful and agreeable women in Florence; and
in order to win her affections he gave a succession of tournaments, feasts,
and banquets, and spared no expense in his entertainments. But this lady,
not less discreet than beautiful, paid no regard to all that was done in her
honor, nor condescended to notice the author of it. Federigo, thus spending all his property, and acquiring none in return, was soon stripped of
his wealth, and became suddenly impoverished, having nothing now ●
remaining but a small farm, on the produce of which he found a bare
subsistence; yet he still retained a favorite falcon, which for her rare
qualities was nowhere to be matched. Being thus unable to live any longer
in the city in the style he was accustomed to, and being more than ever
enamored of the lady, he departed to his little estate in the country, and
there, without inviting anyone to his house, he amused himself with his
falcon, and endured his poverty with tranquil patience. It happened that
when Federigo was reduced to this extremity, the husband of Monna ●
Giovanna fell sick, and feeling the approach of death, made his will,
leaving his possessions, which were very great, to an only son growing up,
and in the event of the son's death, to Monna Giovanna, whom he dearly
loved; and he had no sooner subscribed his will than he died. Monna
Giovanna, having thus become a widow, went according to the custom of
our ladies to pass her year of mourning in retirement, removing to one of
her estates very near to the farm of Federigo.

Recalling Facts

1. Coppo Di Borghese Domenichi took pleasure in
   - ☐ a. telling stories.
   - ☐ b. playing the flute.
   - ☐ c. giving his money away.

2. Federigo was Philippo Alberighi's
   - ☐ a. father.
   - ☐ b. brother.
   - ☐ c. son.

3. In trying to woo Monna Giovanna, Federigo
   - ☐ a. fought with her father.
   - ☐ b. became impoverished.
   - ☐ c. lost his falcon.

4. Monna Giovanna's husband
   - ☐ a. fell sick.
   - ☐ b. moved to the country.
   - ☐ c. hated his son.

5. Monna Giovanna planned to spend a year
   - ☐ a. traveling.
   - ☐ b. writing a book.
   - ☐ c. in mourning.

Understanding the Passage

6. Coppo Di Borghese Domenichi's fame was based on his
   - ☐ a. noble birth.
   - ☐ b. personal achievements.
   - ☐ c. unusual luck.

7. Federigo was an outstanding
   - ☐ a. soldier.
   - ☐ b. philosopher.
   - ☐ c. writer.

8. Monna Giovanna was
   - ☐ a. not easily impressed.
   - ☐ b. separated from her husband.
   - ☐ c. in love with Federigo.

9. After Federigo lost his wealth, he grew to
   - ☐ a. dislike Monna Giovanna.
   - ☐ b. regret ever setting eyes on Monna Giovanna.
   - ☐ c. love Monna Giovanna more than ever.

10. Monna Giovanna's husband really wanted his money to go to
    - ☐ a. his wife.
    - ☐ b. charity.
    - ☐ c. his son.

from **Little Men** *by Louisa May Alcott*

The institution most patronized by all the boys was The Club. It had no other name, and it needed none, being the only one in the neighborhood. The elder lads got it up, and the younger were occasionally admitted if they behaved well. Tommy and Demi were honorary members, but were always obliged to retire unpleasantly early, owing to circumstances over which they had no control. The proceedings of this club were somewhat peculiar, for it met at all sorts of places and hours, had all manner of queer ceremonies and amusements, and now and then was broken up tempestuously, only to be reestablished, however, on a firmer basis.

Rainy evenings the members met in the schoolroom, and passed the time in games: chess, morris, backgammon, fencing matches, recitations, debates, or dramatic performances of a darkly tragical nature. In summer the barn was the rendezvous, and what went on there no uninitiated mortal knows. On sultry evenings the club adjourned to the brook for aquatic exercises, and the members sat about in airy attire, froglike and cool. On such occasions the speeches were unusually eloquent, quite flowing, as one might say; and if any orator's remarks displeased the audience, cold water was thrown upon him till his ardor was effectually quenched. Franz was president, and maintained order admirably, considering the unruly nature of the members. Mr. Bhaer never interfered with their affairs, and was rewarded for this wise forbearance by being invited now and then to behold the mysteries unveiled, which he appeared to enjoy much.

When Nan came, she wished to join the club and caused great excitement and division among the gentlemen by presenting endless petitions, both written and spoken, disturbing their solemnities by insulting them through the keyhole, performing vigorous solos on the door, and writing up derisive remarks on walls and fences, for she belonged to the "Irrepressibles." Finding these appeals vain, the girls, by the advice of Mrs. Jo, got up an institution of their own, which they called The Cozy Club. To this they magnanimously invited the gentlemen whose youth excluded them from the other one, and entertained these favored beings so well with little suppers, new games devised by Nan, and other pleasing festivities that, one by one, the elder boys confessed a desire to partake of these more elegant enjoyments, and, after much consultation, finally decided to propose an interchange of civilities.

Recalling Facts

1. The Club
   - ☐ a. had lots of competition.
   - ☐ b. admitted only older kids.
   - ☐ c. had no other name.

2. Tommy and Demi were
   - ☐ a. regular members.
   - ☐ b. applying for membership.
   - ☐ c. honorary members.

3. During the summer, the rendezvous was the
   - ☐ a. school.
   - ☐ b. woods.
   - ☐ c. barn.

4. When a speaker displeased the audience he was sometimes
   - ☐ a. doused with cold water.
   - ☐ b. booed off the stage.
   - ☐ c. asked to leave the meeting.

5. Nan's attempts to join The Club were
   - ☐ a. successful.
   - ☐ b. futile.
   - ☐ c. halfhearted.

Understanding the Passage

6. Membership in The Club was
   - ☐ a. open to everyone.
   - ☐ b. a highly prized honor.
   - ☐ c. taken for granted.

7. The Club appears to have been
   - ☐ a. breaking up.
   - ☐ b. frowned on by the adults in town.
   - ☐ c. growing stronger.

8. The Club's activities were
   - ☐ a. highly varied.
   - ☐ b. restricted to water sports and chess.
   - ☐ c. immoral as well as illegal.

9. Adults in the town
   - ☐ a. knew little about The Club's activities.
   - ☐ b. sought membership in The Club.
   - ☐ c. monitored The Club's activities closely.

10. Members of The Cozy Club
   - ☐ a. enjoyed Nan's new games.
   - ☐ b. invited young boys over for supper.
   - ☐ c. both a and b.

Though she then gave small promise of commercial eminence, Glasgow was a place of considerable rank and importance. The brimming Clyde, which flows near its walls, gave the means of an inland navigation of some importance. Not only the fertile plains in its immediate neighborhood, but the districts of Ayr and Dumfries, regarded Glasgow as their capital, to which they transmitted their produce, and received in return such necessaries and luxuries as their consumption required.

The dusky mountains of the Western Highlands often sent forth wilder tribes to frequent the marts of St. Mungo's favorite city. Hordes of wild, shaggy, dwarfish cattle and ponies, conducted by Highlanders, as wild, as shaggy, and sometimes as dwarfish as the animals, often traversed the streets of Glasgow. Strangers gazed with surprise on the antique and fantastic dress, and listened to the unknown and dissonant sounds of their language, while the mountaineers, armed even while engaged in this peaceful occupation with musket and pistol, sword, dagger, and target stared with astonishment on the articles of luxury of which they knew not the use, and with an avidity which seemed somewhat alarming on the articles which they knew and valued. It is always with unwillingness that the Highlander quits his deserts, and at this early period it was like tearing a pine from its rock, to plant him elsewhere. Yet even then the mountain glens were over-peopled, although thinned occasionally by famine or by the sword, and many of their inhabitants strayed down to Glasgow—there formed settlements—there sought and found employment, although different, indeed, from that of their native hills. This supply of a hardy and useful population was of consequence to the prosperity of the place, furnished the means of carrying on the few manufactures which the town already boasted, and laid the foundation of its future prosperity.

The exterior of the city corresponded with these promising circumstances. The principal street was broad and important, decorated with public buildings, of an architecture rather striking than correct in point of taste, and running between rows of tall houses, built of stone, the fronts of which were occasionally richly ornamented with masonwork; a circumstance which gave the street an imposing air of dignity and grandeur, of which most English towns are in some measure deprived, by the slight, unsubstantial, and perishable quality and appearance of the bricks with which they are constructed.

Recalling Facts

1. The river which gave Glasgow the means of inland navigation was
   - ☐ a. Clyde.
   - ☐ b. Ayr.
   - ☐ c. Dumfries.

2. The wilder tribes came from the
   - ☐ a. Eastern Plateau.
   - ☐ b. Northern Mountains.
   - ☐ c. Western Highlands.

3. Highlanders often brought into town their
   - ☐ a. sheep.
   - ☐ b. cattle.
   - ☐ c. goats.

4. Even at this time the mountain glens were
   - ☐ a. deserted and barren.
   - ☐ b. suffering a labor shortage.
   - ☐ c. overpopulated.

5. The houses on Glasgow's principal street were made of
   - ☐ a. brick.
   - ☐ b. wood.
   - ☐ c. stone.

Understanding the Passage

6. Glasgow was
   - ☐ a. a key trading center.
   - ☐ b. a commercially unimportant place.
   - ☐ c. the political center of the country.

7. St. Mungo's favorite city was
   - ☐ a. not mentioned.
   - ☐ b. Glasgow.
   - ☐ c. Edinburgh.

8. Highlanders
   - ☐ a. never visited Glasgow.
   - ☐ b. visited Glasgow daily.
   - ☐ c. came to Glasgow from time to time.

9. Highlanders and the residents of Glasgow
   - ☐ a. shared many values and attitudes.
   - ☐ b. had little in common.
   - ☐ c. often fought each other with pistols and swords.

10. Highlanders could best be described as
    - ☐ a. stubborn but practical.
    - ☐ b. wild and extremely violent.
    - ☐ c. polished and personally flexible.

11 *from* **20,000 Leagues under the Sea** *by Jules Verne*

The year 1866 was signalized by a remarkable incident, a mysterious and inexplicable phenomenon, which doubtless no one has yet forgotten. Not to mention rumors which agitated the maritime population, and excited the public mind, even in the interior of continents, seafaring men were particularly excited. Merchants, common sailors, captains of vessels, skippers, both of Europe and America, naval officers of all countries, and the governments of several states on the two continents were deeply interested in the matter.

For some time past, vessels had been met by "an enormous thing," a long object, spindle shaped, occasionally phosphorescent, and infinitely larger ● and more rapid in its movements than a whale.

The facts relating to this apparition (entered in various logbooks) agreed in most respects as to the shape of the object or creature in question, the untiring rapidity of its movements, its surprising power of locomotion, and the peculiar life with which it seemed endowed. If it was a cetacean, it surpassed in size all those hitherto classified in science. Taking into consideration the mean of observations made at divers times—rejecting the timid estimate of those who assigned to this object a length of two hundred feet, equally with the exaggerated opinions which set it down as a mile in width ● and three in length—we might fairly conclude that this mysterious being surpassed greatly all dimensions admitted by the ichthyologists of the day, if it existed at all. And that it did exist was an undeniable fact; and, with that tendency which disposes the human mind in favor of the marvelous, we can understand the excitement produced in the entire world by this supernatural apparition. As to classing it in the list of fable, the idea was out of the question.

On the 20th of July, 1866, the steamer *Governor Higginson*, of the Calcutta ● and Burnach Steam Navigation Company, had met this moving mass five miles off the east coast of Australia. Captain Baker thought at first that he was in the presence of an unknown sandbank; he even prepared to determine its exact position, when two columns of water, projected by the inexplicable object, shot with a hissing noise a hundred and fifty feet up into the air. Now, unless the sandbank had been submitted to the intermittent eruption of a geyser, the *Governor Higginson* had to do neither more nor less than with an aquatic mammal, unknown till then.

Recalling Facts

1. The mysterious phenomenon particularly excited
   - ☐ a. newspaper readers.
   - ☐ b. farmers.
   - ☐ c. seafaring men.

2. Compared to a whale's size, the mysterious phenomenon was
   - ☐ a. slightly smaller.
   - ☐ b. about the same size.
   - ☐ c. infinitely larger.

3. The smallest size estimate was
   - ☐ a. over three miles long.
   - ☐ b. about 200 feet long.
   - ☐ c. nearly 100 feet long.

4. The existence of some strange creature was
   - ☐ a. highly disputed.
   - ☐ b. undeniable.
   - ☐ c. clearly a figment of someone's imagination.

5. The mysterious being had been recently spotted
   - ☐ a. near Calcutta.
   - ☐ b. off the west coast of the United States.
   - ☐ c. off the east coast of Australia.

Understanding the Passage

6. The existence of some strange creature
   - ☐ a. puzzled naval officers.
   - ☐ b. fascinated many governments.
   - ☐ c. concerned only seafaring men.

7. The strange creature had been sighted
   - ☐ a. once.
   - ☐ b. twice.
   - ☐ c. several times.

8. The narrator thought that the mysterious phenomenon
   - ☐ a. belonged in the list of fables.
   - ☐ b. was well known to all ichthyologists.
   - ☐ c. was an understandable source of great excitement.

9. What Captain Baker really saw was
   - ☐ a. a sandbank.
   - ☐ b. another ship.
   - ☐ c. something he couldn't explain.

10. Sandbanks don't usually have
   - ☐ a. an exact position.
   - ☐ b. spouting geysers.
   - ☐ c. an underwater location.

Assuredly a badger is the animal that one most resembles in this trench warfare, that drab-coated creature of the twilight and darkness, digging, burrowing, listening; keeping itself as clean as possible under unfavorable circumstances, fighting tooth and nail on occasion for possession of a few yards of honeycombed earth.

What the badger thinks about life we shall never know, which is a pity, but cannot be helped; it is difficult enough to know what one thinks about, oneself, in the trenches. Parliament, taxes, social gatherings, economies, and expenditure, and all the thousand and one horrors of civilization seem immeasurably remote, and the war itself seems almost as distant and unreal. A couple of hundred yards away, separated from you by a stretch of dismal untidy-looking ground and some strips of rusty wire entanglement, lies a vigilant, bullet-spitting enemy; lurking and watching in those opposing trenches are foemen who might stir the imagination of the most sluggish brain, descendants of the men who went to battle under Moltke, Blücher, Frederick the Great, and the Great Elector, Wallenstein, Maurice of Saxony, Barbarossa, Albert the Bear, Henry the Lion, Witekind the Saxon. They are matched against you there, man for man, in what is perhaps the most stupendous struggle that modern history has known, and yet one thinks remarkably little about them. It would not be advisable to forget for the fraction of a second that they are there, but one's mind does not dwell on their existence; one speculates little as to whether they are drinking warm soup and eating sausage, or going cold and hungry, whether they are well supplied with copies of the *Meggendorfer Blätter* and other light literature or bored with unutterable weariness.

Much more to be thought about than the enemy over yonder or the war over Europe is the mud of the moment, the mud that at times engulfs you as cheese engulfs a cheesemite. In Zoological Gardens one has gazed at a bison loitering at its pleasure more than knee-deep in a quagmire of greasy mud, and one has wondered what it would feel like to be soused and plastered, hour-long, in such a muck bath. One knows now. In narrow-dug support trenches, when thaw and heavy rain have come suddenly atop of a frost, when everything is pitch dark around you, and you can only stumble about and feel your way against streaming mud walls, you understand thoroughly what the bison must experience.

Recalling Facts

1. In this passage, a badger is compared to a man engaged in
   - ☐ a. tribal warfare.
   - ☐ b. total warfare.
   - ☐ c. trench warfare.

2. Like badgers, these soldiers fought over
   - ☐ a. a few yards of dirt.
   - ☐ b. food and water.
   - ☐ c. sleeping arrangements.

3. In this type of warfare, the horrors of civilization seemed
   - ☐ a. close at hand.
   - ☐ b. unthinkable.
   - ☐ c. immeasurably remote.

4. The Great Elector and Barbarossa were
   - ☐ a. military leaders.
   - ☐ b. great scientists.
   - ☐ c. pacifists.

5. The soldiers thought most about
   - ☐ a. the causes of the war.
   - ☐ b. their homeland.
   - ☐ c. the mud.

Understanding the Passage

6. This kind of war was usually fought
   - ☐ a. during daylight hours.
   - ☐ b. on the ground in the darkness.
   - ☐ c. by young children and women.

7. Like the badger, the soldier had a hard time
   - ☐ a. keeping clean.
   - ☐ b. staying out of sight.
   - ☐ c. both a and b.

8. The front lines on the battlefield
   - ☐ a. changed only when hard fought land was won.
   - ☐ b. fluctuated almost every hour.
   - ☐ c. were impossible to draw on a map.

9. The soldiers thought very little about
   - ☐ a. how well the enemy lived.
   - ☐ b. what motivated the enemy.
   - ☐ c. both a and b.

10. The worst conditions for a soldier were
    - ☐ a. hard frosts and snow.
    - ☐ b. thick fog and rain.
    - ☐ c. a quick thaw and heavy rain.

13 *from* **Letter to Erastus Corning and Others** *by Abraham Lincoln*

Prior to my installation as President, it had been inculcated that any State had a lawful right to secede from the national Union, and that it would be expedient to exercise the right whenever the devotees of the doctrine should fail to elect a President to their own liking. I was elected contrary to their liking; and, accordingly, so far as it was legally possible, they had taken seven States out of the Union, had seized many of the United States forts, and had fired upon the United States flag, all before I was inaugurated, and, of course, before I had done any official act whatever. The Rebellion thus begun soon ran into the present Civil War; and, in certain respects, it began on very unequal terms between the parties. The insurgents had been preparing for it more than thirty years, while the Government had taken no steps to resist them. The former had carefully considered all the means which could be turned to their account. It undoubtedly was a well-pondered reliance with them that, in their own unrestricted efforts to destroy Union, Constitution, and law, all together, the Government would, in great degree, be restrained by the same Constitution and law from arresting their progress. Their sympathizers pervaded all departments of the Government and nearly all communities of the people. From this material under cover of "liberty of speech," "liberty of the press," and "habeas corpus," they hoped to keep on foot among us a most efficient corps of spies, informers, suppliers, and aiders and abettors of their cause in a thousand ways. They knew that in times such as they were inaugurating, by the Constitution itself, the "habeas corpus" might be suspended; but they also knew they had friends who would make a question as to *who* was to suspend it; meanwhile, their spies or others might remain at large to help on their cause. Or, if, as has happened, the Executive should suspend the writ, without ruinous waste of time, instances of arresting innocent persons might occur, as are always likely to occur in such cases; and then a clamor could be raised in regard to this, which might be, at least, of some service to the insurgent cause. It needed no very keen perception to discover this part of the enemy's program, so soon as, by open hostilities, their machinery was put in motion.

Recalling Facts

1. At this point, the number of seceding states was
   - ☐ a. five.
   - ☐ b. seven.
   - ☐ c. nine.

2. Before the President was inaugurated,
   - ☐ a. forts were seized.
   - ☐ b. the Union flag was fired upon.
   - ☐ c. both a and b.

3. The insurgents had been preparing for war for
   - ☐ a. 10 years.
   - ☐ b. 20 years.
   - ☐ c. 30 years.

4. The insurgents had sympathizers
   - ☐ a. in all departments of Government.
   - ☐ b. in only a few communities.
   - ☐ c. only in their own territory.

5. The President was most concerned about
   - ☐ a. raising money.
   - ☐ b. public opinion.
   - ☐ c. wasting time.

Understanding the Passage

6. The newly-elected President was
   - ☐ a. widely accepted.
   - ☐ b. very unpopular in some regions.
   - ☐ c. unable to adopt harsh measures.

7. The President felt that the insurgents
   - ☐ a. never gave him a chance.
   - ☐ b. were almost certain to win.
   - ☐ c. had several good Constitutional arguments.

8. The insurgents were
   - ☐ a. well prepared for war.
   - ☐ b. surprised by the outbreak of hostilities.
   - ☐ c. uncertain which road to take.

9. The President thought that the claim of Constitutional rights by sympathizers of the insurgency was
   - ☐ a. logical.
   - ☐ b. emotional.
   - ☐ c. ironic.

10. The President
    - ☐ a. knew exactly what the enemy was doing.
    - ☐ b. felt that time would heal old wounds.
    - ☐ c. agreed never to suspend the writ of habeas corpus.

14 *from* **Richard Savage** *by Samuel Johnson*

In the year 1697, Anne Countess of Macclesfield, having lived some time upon very uneasy terms with her husband, thought a public confession of adultery the most obvious and expeditious method of obtaining her liberty; and therefore declared that the child with which she was then great was begotten by the Earl Rivers. This, as may be imagined, made her husband no less desirous of a separation than herself, and he prosecuted his design in the most effectual manner; for he applied not to the ecclesiastical courts for a divorce, but to the parliament for an act by which his ● marriage might be dissolved, the nuptial contract annulled, and the children of his wife illegitimated. This act, after the usual deliberation, he obtained, though without the approbation of some, who considered marriage as an affair only cognizable by ecclesiastical judges; and, on March 3rd, was separated from his wife, whose fortune—which was very great was repaid her—and who having, as well as her husband, the liberty of making another choice, was in a short time married to Colonel Brett.

While the Earl of Macclesfield was prosecuting this affair, his wife was, on the 10th of January, 1697–8, delivered of a son; and the Earl Rivers, by ● appearing to consider him as his own, left none any reason to doubt of the sincerity of her declaration; for he was his godfather and gave him his own name, which was by his direction inserted in the register of St. Andrew's parish; but, unfortunately, left him to the care of his mother, who, as she was now set free from her husband, he probably imagined likely to treat with great tenderness the child that had contributed to so pleasing an event. It is not indeed easy to discover what motives could be found to ● overbalance that natural affection of a parent, or what interest could be promoted by neglect or cruelty. The dread of shame or poverty cannot be supposed to have affected a woman who had proclaimed her crimes and solicited reproach.

But, whatever her motives, no sooner was her son born than she discovered a resolution of disowning him; and in a very short time removed him from her sight by committing him to the care of a poor woman, who she directed to educate him as her own, and enjoined never to inform him of his true parents.

Recalling Facts

1. Anne Countess of Macclesfield publicly confessed to
   - ☐ a. plagiarism.
   - ☐ b. thievery.
   - ☐ c. adultery.

2. The Earl of Macclesfield took his case to
   - ☐ a. parliament.
   - ☐ b. an ecclesiastical court.
   - ☐ c. the chief magistrate.

3. Anne eventually married
   - ☐ a. the Earl Rivers.
   - ☐ b. Colonel Brett.
   - ☐ c. Richard Savage.

4. The godfather of Anne's son was
   - ☐ a. the Earl Rivers.
   - ☐ b. Colonel Brett.
   - ☐ c. the Earl of Macclesfield.

5. Anne gave her son to
   - ☐ a. the Earl of Macclesfield's new wife.
   - ☐ b. an ecclesiastical orphanage.
   - ☐ c. a poor woman.

Understanding the Passage

6. Anne and the Earl of Macclesfield had
   - ☐ a. an unhappy marriage.
   - ☐ b. neither the blessings of nature nor of fortune.
   - ☐ c. argued almost continuously.

7. The Earl of Macclesfield wanted to sever all ties with
   - ☐ a. Anne.
   - ☐ b. the Macclesfield family.
   - ☐ c. both a and b.

8. The Earl Rivers assumed that Anne would
   - ☐ a. take good care of her new son.
   - ☐ b. soon abandon her son.
   - ☐ c. demand that he relinquish all rights to his son.

9. The narrator could not understand why Anne
   - ☐ a. remarried so quickly.
   - ☐ b. treated her new son so poorly.
   - ☐ c. retained her fortune after her public confessions.

10. Anne showed little love for
   - ☐ a. the Earl of Macclesfield.
   - ☐ b. her new son.
   - ☐ c. both a and b.

15 from The Life and Adventures of Nicholas Nickleby by Charles Dickens

There are many lives of much pain, hardship, and suffering, which, having no stirring interest for any but those who lead them, are disregarded by persons who do not want thought or feeling, but who pamper their compassion and need high stimulants to rouse it.

There are not a few among the disciples of charity who require in their vocation scarcely less excitement than the votaries of pleasure in theirs; and hence it is that diseased sympathy and compassion are everyday expended on out-of-the-way objects, when only too many demands upon the legitimate exercise of the same virtues in a healthy state, are constantly within the sight and hearing of the most unobservant person alive. In short, charity must have its romance, as the novelist or playwright must have his. A thief in fustian is a vulgar character, scarcely to be thought of by persons of refinement; but dress him in green velvet and change the scene of his operations from a thickly peopled city to a mountain road, and you shall find in him the very soul of poetry and adventure. So it is with the one great cardinal virtue, which, properly nourished and exercised, leads to, if it does not necessarily include, all the others. It must have its romance; and the less of real hard struggling workaday life there is in that romance, the better.

The life to which poor Kate Nickleby was devoted, in consequence of the unforeseen train of circumstances already developed in this narrative, was a hard one; but lest the very dullness, unhealthy confinement, and bodily fatigue, which made up its sum and substance, should deprive it of any interest with the mass of the charitable and sympathetic, I would rather keep Miss Nickleby herself in view just now, than chill them by a minute and lengthened description of the establishment presided over by Madame Mantalini.

"Well, now, indeed Madame Mantalini," said Miss Knag, as Kate was making her weary way homewards; "that Miss Nickleby is a very creditable young person—a very creditable young person indeed—hem—upon my word, Madame Mantalini, it does very extraordinary credit even to your discrimination that you should have found such a very excellent, very well-behaved, very—hem—very unassuming young woman to assist in the fitting on. I have seen some young women when they had the opportunity of displaying before their betters, behave so—oh, dear—well."

Recalling Facts

1. According to the narrator, charity needs
   ☐ a. observation.
   ☐ b. romance.
   ☐ c. suffering.

2. Kate Nickleby's life was
   ☐ a. rich.
   ☐ b. hard.
   ☐ c. long.

3. The circumstances of Kate's life were
   ☐ a. told earlier.
   ☐ b. unforeseen.
   ☐ c. both a and b.

4. As Miss Knag began to speak, Kate was
   ☐ a. entering the room.
   ☐ b. talking to Madame Mantalini.
   ☐ c. heading home.

5. Miss Knag described Kate as
   ☐ a. unassuming.
   ☐ b. irresponsible.
   ☐ c. disappointing.

Understanding the Passage

6. The narrator feels that most people show little concern for
   ☐ a. local poor people.
   ☐ b. poor people in far-off places.
   ☐ c. romantic pleasures.

7. According to the narrator, poor people are
   ☐ a. rarely seen.
   ☐ b. everywhere.
   ☐ c. few and far between.

8. The narrator feels that a person's appearance
   ☐ a. should be looked upon with care.
   ☐ b. is the last thing to judge a person by.
   ☐ c. has something to do with how they are valued.

9. The narrator believes that most charitable and sympathetic people would
   ☐ a. ignore Kate.
   ☐ b. help Kate.
   ☐ c. adore Kate.

10. Miss Knag's description of Kate appears to be
    ☐ a. heartfelt and sincere.
    ☐ b. modest and well balanced.
    ☐ c. condescending and overblown.

I assured the Marquis de Lafayette of the men's welcome. When they arrived they were Lafayette himself, Duport, Barnave, Alexander la Meth, Blacon, Mounier, Maubourg, and Dagout. These were leading Patriots, of honest but differing opinions, sensible of the necessity of effecting a coalition by mutual sacrifices, knowing each other, and not afraid, therefore, to unbosom themselves mutually. This last was a material principle in the selection. With this view the Marquis had invited the conference, and had fixed the time and place inadvertently, as to the embarrassment under which it might place me. The cloth being removed, and wine set on the table after the American manner, the Marquis introduced the objects of the conference by summarily reminding them of the state of things in the Assembly, the course which the principles of the Constitution were taking, and the inevitable result, unless checked by more concord among the Patriots themselves. He observed, that although he also had his opinion, he was ready to sacrifice it to that of his brethren of the same cause; but that a common opinion must now be formed, or the Aristocracy would carry everything, and that, whatever they should now agree on, he, at the head of the national force, would maintain. The discussions began at the hour of four, and were continued till ten o'clock in the evening; during which time I was a silent witness to a coolness and candor of argument, unusual in the conflicts of political opinion; to a logical reasoning, and chaste eloquence, disfigured by no gaudy tinsel of rhetoric or declamation, and truly worthy of being placed in parallel with the finest dialogues of antiquity, as handed to us by Xenophon, by Plato, and Cicero. The result was that the King should have a suspensive veto on the laws, that the legislature should be composed of a single body only, and that chosen by the people. This *Concordat* decided the fate of the Constitution. The Patriots all rallied to the principles thus settled, carried every question agreeably to them, and reduced the aristocracy to insignificance and impotence. But duties of exculpation were now incumbent on me. I waited on Count Montmorin the next morning, and explained to him with truth and candor how it happened that my house had been made the scene of conferences of such a character. He told me he already knew everything which had passed.

Recalling Facts

1. The conference members
   - ☐ a. knew each other well.
   - ☐ b. were not willing to compromise.
   - ☐ c. had nothing in common.

2. The man responsible for arranging the conference was
   - ☐ a. the narrator.
   - ☐ b. the Marquis de Lafayette.
   - ☐ c. Dagout.

3. The discussions lasted about
   - ☐ a. six hours.
   - ☐ b. twelve hours.
   - ☐ c. two days.

4. The men decided that the king would be given
   - ☐ a. a pocket veto.
   - ☐ b. a suspensive veto.
   - ☐ c. no veto power.

5. The house used for the conference belonged to
   - ☐ a. the narrator.
   - ☐ b. Count Montmorin.
   - ☐ c. Cicero.

Understanding the Passage

6. The Patriots' mission was to
   - ☐ a. topple the king.
   - ☐ b. strike a workable compromise.
   - ☐ c. get themselves elected to high offices.

7. Apparently, the place chosen for the conference was
   - ☐ a. not chosen intentionally
   - ☐ b. strongly supported by the narrator.
   - ☐ c. defended by the aristocracy.

8. Unlike the others, the narrator
   - ☐ a. loved to argue.
   - ☐ b. refused to compromise.
   - ☐ c. remained silent during the discussions.

9. Apparently, the Patriots' greatest enemy was
   - ☐ a. the king.
   - ☐ b. the aristocracy.
   - ☐ c. meddling foreigners.

10. The narrator believed that most political discussions were
    - ☐ a. not calm, but highly passionate.
    - ☐ b. conducted by calm and clearheaded men.
    - ☐ c. worthless.

The university was charming, an unforgettable place. It was situated in the little village of Pulpit Hill, in the central midland of the big state. Students came and departed by motor from the dreary tobacco town of Exeter, twelve miles away. The countryside was raw, powerful, and ugly, a rolling land of field, wood, and hollow; but the university itself was buried in a pastoral wilderness, on a long tabling butte, which rose steeply above the country. One burst suddenly, at the hilltop, on the end of the straggling village street, flanked by faculty houses, and winding a mile into the town center and the university. The central campus sloped back and up over a broad area of rich turf, groved with magnificent ancient trees. A quadrangle of post-Revolutionary buildings of weathered brick bounded the upper end: other newer buildings, in the modern bad manner (the Pedagogic Neo-Greeky), were scattered around beyond the central design: beyond, there was a thickly forested wilderness. There was still a good flavor of the wilderness about the place—one felt its remoteness, its isolated charm. It seemed to Eugene like a provincial outpost of great Rome: the wilderness crept up to it like a beast.

Few of the university's sons had been distinguished in the nation's life—there had been an obscure president of the United States, and a few Cabinet members, but few had sought such distinction: it was glory enough to be a great man in one's state. Nothing beyond mattered very much.

In this pastoral setting a young man was enabled to loaf comfortably and delightfully through four luxurious and indolent years. There was, God knows, seclusion enough for monastic scholarship, but the rare romantic quality of the atmosphere, the prodigal opulence of springtime, thick with flowers and drenched in a fragrant warmth of green shimmering light, quenched pretty thoroughly any incipient rash of bookishness. Instead, they loafed and invited their souls or, with great energy and enthusiasm, promoted the affairs of glee clubs, athletic teams, class politics, fraternities, debating societies, and dramatic clubs. And they talked—always they talked, under the trees, against the ivied walls, assembled in their rooms, they talked—in limp sprawls—incessant, charming, empty Southern talk; they talked with a large easy fluency about God, the Devil, and philosophy, the girls, politics, athletics, fraternities and the girls—my God! How they talked!

Recalling Facts

1. The university was located
   - ☐ a. along the state's coastline.
   - ☐ b. in the western mountains of the state.
   - ☐ c. in the central midland of the state.

2. Exeter was a
   - ☐ a. tobacco town.
   - ☐ b. college town.
   - ☐ c. Revolutionary battleground.

3. To Eugene, the university seemed like a
   - ☐ a. Roman outpost.
   - ☐ b. Greek fantasy.
   - ☐ c. pulsating metropolis.

4. One graduate went on to become
   - ☐ a. a Supreme Court justice.
   - ☐ b. the Speaker of the House of Representatives.
   - ☐ c. the President of the United States.

5. The major activity on campus was
   - ☐ a. reading books.
   - ☐ b. attending lectures.
   - ☐ c. talking.

Understanding the Passage

6. The university appears to be
   - ☐ a. a brand-new school.
   - ☐ b. an old, well-established institution.
   - ☐ c. within a short commute of surrounding towns.

7. Apparently, students at the university did not
   - ☐ a. enjoy themselves.
   - ☐ b. leave campus very often.
   - ☐ c. have adequate facilities.

8. The highest glory fell to the graduates who became
   - ☐ a. Cabinet officers.
   - ☐ b. state officials.
   - ☐ c. military officers.

9. Life at the university could best be described as
   - ☐ a. relaxed and easygoing.
   - ☐ b. an intellectual grind.
   - ☐ c. highly disciplined and regimented.

10. Graduates of this university apparently were well trained in
    - ☐ a. writing skills.
    - ☐ b. social skills.
    - ☐ c. debating skills.

Wilhelm, Count Berlifitzing, although loftily descended, was, at the epoch of this narrative, an infirm and doting old man remarkable for nothing but an inordinate and inveterate personal antipathy to the family of his rival, and so passionate a love of horses and of hunting that neither bodily infirmity, great age, nor mental incapacity prevented his daily participation in the dangers of the chase.

Frederick, Baron Metzengerstein, was, on the other hand, not yet of age. In a city eighteen years are no long period; but in a wilderness, in so magnificent a wilderness as that old principality, the pendulum vibrates with a deeper meaning.

From some peculiar circumstances attending the administration of his father, the young baron, at the decease of the former, entered immediately upon his vast possessions. His castles were without number: the chief in point of splendor and extent was the Palace Metzengerstein. The boundary line of his dominions was never clearly defined, but his principal park embraced a circuit of fifty miles.

Upon the succession of a proprietor so young, with a character so well known, to a fortune so unparalleled, little speculation was afloat in regard to his probable course of conduct. And, indeed, for the space of three days the behavior of the heir out Heroded Herod, and fairly surpassed the expectations of his most enthusiastic admirers. Shameful debaucheries, flagrant treacheries, unheard-of atrocities, gave his trembling vassals quickly to understand that no servile submission on their part, no punctilios of conscience on his own, were thenceforward to prove any security against the remorseless fangs of a petty Caligula. On the night of the fourth day the stables of the Castle Berlifitzing were discovered to be on fire, and the unanimous opinion of the neighborhood added the crime of the incendiary to the already hideous list of the Baron's misdemeanors and enormities.

But during the tumult occasioned by this occurrence the young nobleman himself sat apparently buried in meditation, in a vast and desolate upper apartment of the family palace of Metzengerstein. The rich although faded tapestry hangings which swung gloomily upon the walls represented the shadowy and majestic forms of a thousand illustrious ancestors. Here, rich-ermined priests and pontifical dignitaries, familiarly seated with the autocrat and the sovereign, put a veto on the wishes of a temporal king or restrained with the fiat of papal supremacy the rebellious scepter of the archenemy.

Recalling Facts

1. Count Berlifitzing had a passionate love for
   - □ a. horses.
   - □ b. dancing.
   - □ c. debating.

2. Baron Metzengerstein was
   - □ a. 18 years old.
   - □ b. middle-aged.
   - □ c. extremely old.

3. The Baron's most impressive castle was the
   - □ a. Castle Berlifitzing.
   - □ b. Palace Metzengerstein.
   - □ c. Herod Castle.

4. One night the stables of the Castle Berlifitzing
   - □ a. were raided.
   - □ b. caught fire.
   - □ c. suddenly collapsed.

5. On the night of the fourth day of his reign, the Baron was
   - □ a. buried in meditation.
   - □ b. committing various atrocities.
   - □ c. traveling to see the count.

Understanding the Passage

6. The count and the baron were not
   - □ a. friends.
   - □ b. related.
   - □ c. neighbors.

7. Count Berlifitzing apparently had a great
   - □ a. collection of animals.
   - □ b. capacity for hatred.
   - □ c. love for his neighbors.

8. "The pendulum vibrates with a deeper meaning" refers to the
   - □ a. growth of the clock-making industry.
   - □ b. joys of country living.
   - □ c. passage of time.

9. The young baron quickly acted as if he were
   - □ a. a promising young leader.
   - □ b. incapable of taking decisive action.
   - □ c. a cross between a tyrant and a despot.

10. The neighbors suspected that the arsonist was
    - □ a. a visiting priest.
    - □ b. the baron.
    - □ c. the count.

19   *from* **Humphrey Clinker** *by Tobias Smollett*

I think those people are unreasonable, who complain that Bath is a contracted circle, in which the same dull scenes perpetually revolve, without variation—I am, on the contrary, amazed to find so small a place so crowded with entertainment and variety. London itself can hardly exhibit one species of diversion, to which we have not something analogous at Bath, over and above those singular advantages that are peculiar to the place. Here, for example, a man has daily opportunities of seeing the most remarkable characters of the community. He sees them in their natural attitudes and true colors; descended from their pedestals, and divested of their formal draperies, undisguised by art and affectation—Here we have ministers of state, judges, generals, bishops, promoters, philosophers, wits, poets, players, *chemists, fiddlers,* and *buffoons.* If he makes any considerable stay in the place, he is sure of meeting with some particular friend, whom he did not expect to see; and to me there is nothing more agreeable than such casual rencounters—Another entertainment, peculiar to Bath, arises from the general mixture of all degrees assembled in our public rooms, without distinction of rank or fortune. This is what my uncle condemns, as a monstrous jumble of heterogeneous principles; a vile mob of noise and impertinence, without decency or subordination. But this chaos is to me a source of infinite amusement.

I was extremely diverted last ball night to see the Master of Ceremonies leading, with great solemnity, an antiquated Abigail, dressed in her lady's cast-off clothes; whom he (I suppose) mistook for some countess just arrived at Bath. The ball was opened by a Scotch lord, with a mulatto heiress from St. Christopher's; and the gay colonel Tinsel danced all the evening with the daughter of an eminent tinman from the borough of Southwark. Yesterday morning, at the Pump Room, I saw a broken-winded Wapping landlady squeeze through a circle of peers, to salute her brandy merchant, who stood by the window, propped upon crutches; and a paralytic attorney of Shoe Lane, in shuffling up to the bar, kicked the shins of the chancellor of England, while his lordship, in a cut bob, drank a glass of water at the pump. I cannot account for my being pleased with these incidents, any other way, than by saying they are truly ridiculous in their own nature, and serve to heighten the humor in the farce of life.

Recalling Facts

1. The narrator found Bath
   - ☐ a. too democratic.
   - ☐ b. dull.
   - ☐ c. lively.

2. One distinctive feature of Bath was
   - ☐ a. the mixing of all classes in the public rooms.
   - ☐ b. the absence of philosophers and poets.
   - ☐ c. its rigid class structure.

3. The narrator's uncle did not enjoy
   - ☐ a. chaos.
   - ☐ b. solitude.
   - ☐ c. politics.

4. The ball was opened by
   - ☐ a. an antiquated Abigail.
   - ☐ b. a Scotch noble.
   - ☐ c. an army colonel.

5. The chancellor of England was drinking a glass of
   - ☐ a. water.
   - ☐ b. beer.
   - ☐ c. brandy.

Understanding the Passage

6. Apparently, Bath
   - ☐ a. had its share of critics.
   - ☐ b. was too small to draw much attention.
   - ☐ c. attracted only certain kinds of people.

7. The activities at Bath promoted
   - ☐ a. political injustice.
   - ☐ b. social equality.
   - ☐ c. economic stability.

8. If Bath had a slogan, it might be:
   - ☐ a. "Working men of the world, unite!"
   - ☐ b. "It takes all kinds to make a world."
   - ☐ c. "A chicken in every pot

9. The narrator's uncle apparently came from
   - ☐ a. a working class family.
   - ☐ b. the suburbs of London.
   - ☐ c. an upper-class family.

10. The ball
    - ☐ a. mystified the narrator.
    - ☐ b. appalled the narrator.
    - ☐ c. delighted the narrator.

The month of May had already commenced, and I expected the letter daily which was to establish the date of my departure, when Henry proposed a pedestrian tour in the environs of Ingolstadt, that I might bid a personal farewell to the country I had so long inhabited. I acceded with pleasure to this proposition: I was fond of exercise, and Henry had always been my favorite companion in the rambles of this nature that I had taken among the scenes of my native country.

We passed a fortnight in these perambulations: my health and spirits had long been restored, and they gained additional strength from the salubrious air I breathed, the natural incidents of our progress, and the conversation of my friend. Study had previously secluded me from the intercourse of my fellow creatures, and rendered me unsocial; but Henry called forth the better feelings of my heart; he again taught me to love the aspect of nature, and the cheerful faces of children. Excellent friend! How sincerely did you care for me, and endeavor to elevate my mind until it was on a level with your own! A selfish pursuit had cramped and narrowed me, until your gentleness and affection warmed and opened my senses; I became the same happy creature who, a few years ago, loved and beloved by all, had no sorrow or care. When happy, inanimate nature had the power of bestowing on me absolutely delightful sensations: a serene sky and verdant fields could fill me with ecstasy. The present season was indeed divine; the flowers of spring bloomed in hedges, while those of summer were already in bud. I was undisturbed by thoughts which during the preceding year had pressed upon me, notwithstanding my endeavors to throw them off, with an invincible burden.

Henry rejoiced in my gaiety, and sincerely sympathized in my feelings: he exerted himself to entertain me, while he expressed the sensations that filled his soul. The resources of his mind on this occasion were truly astonishing: his conversation was full of imagination; and very often, in imitation of the Persian and Arabic writers, he invented tales of wonderful fancy and passion. At other times he repeated my favorite poems, or drew me out into arguments, which he supported with great ingenuity.

We returned to our college on a Sunday afternoon: the peasants were dancing, and everyone we met appeared gay and happy.

Recalling Facts

1. The narrator was expecting a
   - ☐ a. funeral.
   - ☐ b. visitor.
   - ☐ c. letter.

2. Henry and the narrator toured Ingolstadt
   - ☐ a. on foot.
   - ☐ b. by carriage.
   - ☐ c. on horseback.

3. During the trip around Ingolstadt, the narrator
   - ☐ a. became more and more unsocial.
   - ☐ b. lost all sense of time and place.
   - ☐ c. became happier and more carefree.

4. To amuse the narrator, Henry
   - ☐ a. told imaginative stories.
   - ☐ b. painted the faces of children.
   - ☐ c. imitated Persian and Arabic leaders.

5. After traveling, the narrator and Henry returned to their
   - ☐ a. home.
   - ☐ b. college.
   - ☐ c. professions.

Understanding the Passage

6. The narrator and Henry had
   - ☐ a. just recently met.
   - ☐ b. known each other for a long time.
   - ☐ c. been in Ingolstadt only a few days.

7. Henry was apparently very
   - ☐ a. intelligent and energetic.
   - ☐ b. shy and withdrawn.
   - ☐ c. cynical and morose.

8. During the preceding year, the narrator had been
   - ☐ a. worried and preoccupied.
   - ☐ b. immersed in a love of nature.
   - ☐ c. conversing with artists of all varieties.

9. The narrator believed that Henry was
   - ☐ a. a true friend.
   - ☐ b. struggling to overcome his sorrow.
   - ☐ c. anxious to complete the trip.

10. The narrator felt the tour of Ingolstadt was
    - ☐ a. a disappointment.
    - ☐ b. surprisingly inexpensive.
    - ☐ c. rejuvenating.

Lucien's death and the invasion of the Conciergerie by Madame de Serizy had produced such disturbance to the running gear of that machine that the director had forgotten to release the Spanish priest from the secret cells.

Though there is more than one instance in judiciary annals of the death of an accused person during the preliminary examination of a case, it is sufficiently rare to force the warders, clerks, and the director himself out of the usual calmness with which they perform their duties. And yet, to their minds, the great event was not that a fine young man was suddenly ● a corpse, but that a wrought iron bar at their gateway had been broken by the delicate hands of a fashionable woman. No sooner, therefore, had the attorney general, Comte Octave de Bauvan, and the Comte de Servizy, carried off the fainting countess in the latter's carriage, then the director and all his assistants, together with Monsieur Lebrun, the prison doctor (called to certify the young man's death, in company with the "death doctor" of the administrative subdivision in which Lucien lived), collected about the iron gate to examine it.

We may mention here that in Paris the "death doctor" is a physician whose ● business it is in each administrative subdivision to verify all deaths, and examine into their causes.

With the rapidity of judgment which distinguished him, Monsieur de Granville had seen that it was necessary, for the honor of the three families concerned, that Lucien's death should be certified to in the administrative subdivision of the Quai Malaquais, where he had lived; and that the funeral procession should proceed from his own house to the parish church, Saint-Germain des Pres, where the services were to be held. Monsieur de Chargeboeuf, Monsieur de Granville's secretary, sent by him, had orders ● to that effect. The removal of Lucien's body from the prison to his late home was to take place during the night. To all the world, therefore, Lucien would seem to have died in his own house, where his friends were invited to assemble to attend his funeral.

Therefore, at the moment when Camusot, with a mind relieved, was sitting down to table with his ambitious better half, the director of the Conciergerie, the prison doctor, and the death doctor were standing outside the iron railing, deploring the fragility of iron bars and discussing the extraordinary strength of nervous women.

Recalling Facts

1. The director of the Conciergerie forgot to
   - ☐ a. pardon Lucien.
   - ☐ b. arrest Madame de Serizy.
   - ☐ c. release the Spanish priest.

2. The death of an accused person during the preliminary examination of a case was
   - ☐ a. unheard of.
   - ☐ b. quite rare.
   - ☐ c. fairly common.

3. Madame de Serizy had broken a
   - ☐ a. wrought iron bar.
   - ☐ b. prison window.
   - ☐ c. guard's nightstick.

4. Quai Malaquais was
   - ☐ a. the death doctor.
   - ☐ b. an administrative district.
   - ☐ c. the funeral director.

5. Lucien's body was removed from the prison during the
   - ☐ a. morning.
   - ☐ b. afternoon.
   - ☐ c. night.

Understanding the Passage

6. Monsieur de Granville wanted to
   - ☐ a. protect the reputation of Lucien's family.
   - ☐ b. punish Lucien's family.
   - ☐ c. meet the members of Lucien's family.

7. Lucien's death was notable because of
   - ☐ a. the value of the murder weapon.
   - ☐ b. its time and place.
   - ☐ c. his connections with criminals.

8. The prison authorities were most interested in the
   - ☐ a. broken iron bar.
   - ☐ b. young man's body.
   - ☐ c. reaction of the press.

9. The removal of Lucien's body from the prison was done
   - ☐ a. brazenly.
   - ☐ b. maliciously.
   - ☐ c. discreetly.

10. The people around the iron railing were
    - ☐ a. amazed that the iron bar had been broken.
    - ☐ b. relieved that the iron bar had finally been bent.
    - ☐ c. searching for the missing iron bar.

from **Billy Budd** *by Herman Melville*

Very little in the manner of the men and nothing obvious in the demeanor of the officers would have suggested to an ordinary observer that the Great Mutiny was a recent event. In their general bearing and conduct the commissioned officers of a warship naturally take their tone from the commander, that is if he has that ascendancy of character that ought to be his.

Captain the Honorable Edward Fairfax Vere, to give his full title, was a bachelor of forty or thereabouts, a sailor of distinction even in a time prolific of renowned seamen. Though allied to the higher nobility his advancement had not been altogether owing to influences connected with that circumstance. He had seen much service, been in various engagements, always acquitting himself as an officer mindful of the welfare of his men, but never tolerating an infraction of discipline; thoroughly versed in the science of his profession, and intrepid to the verge of temerity, though never injudiciously so. For his gallantry in the West Indian waters as flag lieutenant under Rodney in that admiral's crowning victory over De Grasse, he was made a post captain.

Ashore in the garb of a civilian scarce anyone would have taken him for a sailor, more especially that he never garnished unprofessional talk with nautical terms, and, grave in his bearing, evinced little appreciation of mere humor. It was not out of keeping with these traits that on a passage when nothing demanded his paramount action, he was the most undemonstrative of men. Any landsman observing this gentleman not conspicuous by his stature and wearing no pronounced insignia, emerging from his cabin to the open deck, and noting the silent deference of the officers retiring to leeward, might have taken him for the King's guest, a civilian aboard the King's ship, some highly honorable discreet envoy on his way to an important post. But in fact this unobtrusiveness of demeanor may have proceeded from a certain unaffected modesty of manhood sometimes accompanying a resolute nature, a modesty evinced at all times not calling for pronounced action, and which, shown in any rank of life, suggests a virtue aristocratic in kind.

As with some others engaged in various departments of the world's more heroic activities, Captain Vere, though practical enough upon occasion, would at times betray a certain dreaminess of mood.

Recalling Facts

1. The Great Mutiny had occurred
   - ☐ a. on a different ship.
   - ☐ b. recently.
   - ☐ c. in West Indian waters.

2. Edward Vere was
   - ☐ a. a sea captain.
   - ☐ b. a bachelor.
   - ☐ c. both a and b.

3. Vere was promoted for his gallantry in the victory over
   - ☐ a. De Grasse.
   - ☐ b. Rodney.
   - ☐ c. Melville.

4. Before his promotion, Vere was
   - ☐ a. a post captain.
   - ☐ b. an ordinary seaman.
   - ☐ c. a flag lieutenant.

5. Vere had little appreciation for
   - ☐ a. nobility.
   - ☐ b. modesty.
   - ☐ c. mere humor.

Understanding the Passage

6. Vere's advancement in the navy was due largely to
   - ☐ a. friends in high places.
   - ☐ b. courage under fire.
   - ☐ c. his humble origins.

7. Vere was
   - ☐ a. an easygoing captain.
   - ☐ b. unconcerned about the welfare of his men.
   - ☐ c. a strict disciplinarian.

8. On shore, Vere rarely talked to ordinary people about
   - ☐ a. naval affairs.
   - ☐ b. the nature of men.
   - ☐ c. religion.

9. At sea, Vere was usually
   - ☐ a. quiet and reserved.
   - ☐ b. high-strung.
   - ☐ c. dashing and boastful.

10. While practical, Vere sometimes seemed to
    - ☐ a. be slightly unbalanced.
    - ☐ b. be angry at the world.
    - ☐ c. allow his thoughts to wander.

The warriors arose from their place of brief rest and simple refreshment, and courteously aided each other while they carefully replaced and adjusted the harness from which they had relieved for the time their trusty steeds. Each seemed familiar with an employment which at that time was a part of necessary and, indeed, of indispensable duty. Each also seemed to possess, as far as the difference betwixt the animal and rational species admitted, the confidence and affection of the horse which was the constant companion of his travels and his warfare. With the Saracen this familiar intimacy was a part of his early habits; for, in the tents of the Eastern military tribes, the horse of the soldier ranks next to, and almost equal in importance with, his wife and his family; and, with the European warrior, circumstances, and indeed necessity, rendered his war-horse scarcely less than his brother-in-arms. The steeds, therefore, suffered themselves quietly to be taken from their food and liberty, and neighed and snuffled fondly around their masters, while they were adjusting their accoutrements for farther travel and additional toil. And each warrior, as he prosecuted his own task, or assisted with courtesy his companion, looked with observant curiosity at the equipments of his fellow traveler, and noted particularly what struck him as peculiar in the fashion in which he arranged his riding accoutrements.

Ere they remounted to resume their journey, the Christian knight again moistened his lips, and dipped his hands in the living fountain, and said to his pagan associate of the journey, "I would I knew the name of this delicious fountain, that I might hold it in my grateful remembrance; for never did water slake more deliciously a more oppressive thirst than I have this day experienced."

"It is called in the Arabic language," answered the Saracen, "by a name which signifies the Diamond of the Desert."

"And well is it so named," replied the Christian. "My native valley hath a thousand springs, but not to one of them shall I attach hereafter such precious recollection as to this solitary fount, which bestows its liquid treasures where they are not only delightful, but nearly indispensable."

"You say truth," said the Saracen; "for the curse is still on yonder sea of death, and neither man nor beast drinks of its waves, nor of the river which feeds without filling it, until this inhospitable desert be passed."

Recalling Facts

1. In Eastern military tribes, a soldier's horse is considered
   □ a. very important.
   □ b. a necessary evil.
   □ c. a sign of wealth.

2. In this passage, the warriors prepared their horses for
   □ a. additional travel.
   □ b. a long rest.
   □ c. sale in the marketplace.

3. The Christian knight praised
   □ a. the Saracen's religious tradition.
   □ b. the landowner who let them camp for the night.
   □ c. the quality of the water in the fountain.

4. The Christian knight's native valley contained
   □ a. a vast desert.
   □ b. thousands of palm trees.
   □ c. many springs.

5. Ahead of the warriors was
   □ a. a "sea of death."
   □ b. a tribe called the "Diamond of the Desert."
   □ c. the Christian knight's hometown.

Understanding the Passage

6. The warriors knew how to
   □ a. construct a sturdy shelter.
   □ b. handle their horses.
   □ c. sail on the Sea of Death

7. The warriors treated each other with
   □ a. suspicion.
   □ b. hostility.
   □ c. respect.

8. The Saracen had
   □ a. European ancestors.
   □ b. an Arab background.
   □ c. an English education.

9. The Saracen was not a
   □ a. warrior.
   □ b. Christian.
   □ c. horseman.

10. Traveling through the desert made the warriors
    □ a. self-confident.
    □ b. thirsty.
    □ c. wary.

Elena received Berseneff in a friendly manner, not in the garden, but in the drawing room, and immediately, almost impatiently, renewed their conversation of the previous evening. She was alone: Nikolai Artemievitch had quietly slipped off somewhere; Anna Vasilievna was lying down upstairs with a wet compress on her head. Zoya was sitting beside her, with her skirt primly arranged, and her hands folded on her knees; Uvar Ivanovitch was reposing in the mezzanine on a broad, comfortable divan, which had received the nickname of "the doze compeller." Again Berseneff alluded to his father: he held his memory sacred. Let us say a few words about him. ●

The owner of eighty-two male serfs, whom he emancipated before his death, an "enlightened" person, a former student at Göttingen, the author of a manuscript work, "The Presentations or Prefigurings of the Soul in the World," a work wherein Schellingism, Swedenborgianism, and republicanism were intermingled in the most original manner—Berseneff's father brought him to Moscow while he was still a small lad, immediately after the death of his mother, and himself undertook his education. He prepared himself for every lesson, and toiled with remarkable conscientiousness and with utter lack of success: he was a dreamer, a bookworm, a mystic, ● he talked with a stutter, in a dull voice, expressed himself obscurely and in an involved way, chiefly in comparisons, and was abashed even in the presence of his son, whom he passionately loved. It is not surprising that the son was merely staggered by his lessons, and did not advance a hair's breadth. The old man (he was about fifty years of age, having married very late in life) divined, at last, that things were not going as they should, and placed his Andriusha in a boarding school. Andriusha began to learn, but ● did not escape from parental oversight: the father visited him incessantly, boring the head of the school to death with his exhortations and conversations; the inspectors also were bored by the unbidden visitor: he was constantly bringing them what they called most amazing books on education. Even the scholars felt uncomfortable at the sight of the old man's tanned and pockmarked face, his gaunt figure, constantly clad in a spike-tailed grey dress coat. The schoolboys never suspected that this surly gentleman, who never smiled, with his storklike gait and long nose, heartily sympathized and grieved with every one of them.

Recalling Facts

1. Elena received Berseneff in the
   - ☐ a. drawing room.
   - ☐ b. garden.
   - ☐ c. dining room.

2. Uvar Ivanovitch was
   - ☐ a. lying down with a wet compress on his head.
   - ☐ b. resting on the divan.
   - ☐ c. sitting beside Anna.

3. Berseneff's father once had eighty-two
   - ☐ a. race horses.
   - ☐ b. acres of land.
   - ☐ c. male serfs.

4. Berseneff's father brought him as a young child to live in
   - ☐ a. Göttingen.
   - ☐ b. Sweden.
   - ☐ c. Moscow.

5. Berseneff's father placed his son in a
   - ☐ a. public school.
   - ☐ b. military school.
   - ☐ c. boarding school.

Understanding the Passage

6. The previous evening, Elena had been
   - ☐ a. sick in bed.
   - ☐ b. talking with Berseneff.
   - ☐ c. visiting her son's school

7. Berseneff
   - ☐ a. worshipped his father.
   - ☐ b. barely remembered his father.
   - ☐ c. loathed his father.

8. Berseneff's father could best be described as
   - ☐ a. a hero.
   - ☐ b. an eccentric.
   - ☐ c. a pragmatist.

9. Berseneff's father was a poor
   - ☐ a. scholar.
   - ☐ b. speaker.
   - ☐ c. father.

10. The visits which Berseneff's father made to the school
    - ☐ a. annoyed the teachers.
    - ☐ b. puzzled the teachers.
    - ☐ c. surprised the teachers.

Mrs. Ludlow was the eldest of the three sisters, and was usually considered the most sensible; the classification being in general that Lilian was the practical one, Edith the beauty and Isabel the "intellectual" superior. Mrs. Keyes, the second of the group, was the wife of an officer of the United States Engineers, and as our history is not further concerned with her it will suffice that she was indeed extremely pretty and that she formed the ornament of those various military stations, chiefly in the unfashionable West, to which, to her deep chagrin, her husband was successively relegated. Lilian had married a New York lawyer, a young man with an extraordinarily loud voice and an obvious enthusiasm for his profession; the match was not brilliant, any more than Edith's, but Lilian had occasionally been spoken of as a young woman who might be thankful to marry at all— she was so much plainer than her sisters. She was, however, very happy, and now, as the mother of two peremptory little boys and the mistress of a wedge of brownstone violently driven into Fifty-third Street, seemed to exult in her condition. She was short and solid, and her claim to figure was questionable, but she was conceded presence, though not majesty; she had moreover, as people said, improved since her marriage, and the two things in life of which she was most distinctly conscious were her husband's force in argument and her sister Isabel's originality. "I've never kept up with Isabel—it would have taken *all* my time," she had often remarked; in spite of which, however, she held her rather wistfully in sight; watching her as a motherly spaniel might watch a free greyhound. "I simply want to see her safely married—that's what I want to see," she frequently noted to her husband.

"Well, I must say I should have no particular desire to marry her," Edmund Ludlow was accustomed to answer in an extremely audible tone.

"I know you say that for argument; you always take the opposite ground; but I don't understand what you've against her except that she's so original."

"Well, I don't like originals; I like translations," Mr. Ludlow had more than once replied. "Isabel's written in a foreign tongue. She ought to marry a foreigner."

"That's exactly what I'm afraid she'll do!" cried Lilian, who thought Isabel capable of anything.

Recalling Facts

1. Edith had the reputation of being
   - ☐ a. intellectual.
   - ☐ b. nasty.
   - ☐ c. beautiful.

2. Lilian's husband worked as
   - ☐ a. an army engineer.
   - ☐ b. a lawyer.
   - ☐ c. a translator.

3. Mrs. Ludlow wanted to see Isabel
   - ☐ a. move to New York.
   - ☐ b. get married.
   - ☐ c. travel abroad.

4. Lilian was the mother of
   - ☐ a. a baby boy.
   - ☐ b. two little boys.
   - ☐ c. three little boys.

5. Mr. Ludlow said he thought Isabel should
   - ☐ a. give up on the idea of marriage.
   - ☐ b. marry a foreigner.
   - ☐ c. marry a native New Yorker.

Understanding the Passage

6. Mrs. Ludlow thought Isabel was
   - ☐ a. unpredictable.
   - ☐ b. unappreciative.
   - ☐ c. unfashionable.

7. Mr. Ludlow was not
   - ☐ a. in favor of moving to New York.
   - ☐ b. happy with his profession.
   - ☐ c. attracted by Isabel's personality.

8. Apparently, Mrs. Keyes was
   - ☐ a. thrilled to be living in the West.
   - ☐ b. not on speaking terms with her sisters.
   - ☐ c. a minor figure in this story.

9. Lilian was not considered
   - ☐ a. physically attractive.
   - ☐ b. a loyal sister.
   - ☐ c. realistic.

10. Compared to Isabel, Lilian's life appeared to be
    - ☐ a. in shambles.
    - ☐ b. filled with surprises.
    - ☐ c. sedate and well ordered

Throughout Giovanni Guasconti's whole acquaintance with Beatrice, he had occasionally, as we have said, been haunted by dark surmises as to her character. Yet, so thoroughly had she made herself felt by him as a simple, natural, most affectionate and guileless creature, that the image now held up by Professor Baglioni looked as strange and incredible as if it were not in accordance with his own original conception. True, there were ugly recollections connected with his first glimpse of the beautiful girl; he could not quite forget the bouquet that withered in her grasp, and the insect that perished amid the sunny air, by no ostensible agency save the fragrance of her breath. These incidents, however, dissolving in the pure light of her character, had no longer the efficacy of facts, but were acknowledged as mistaken fantasies, by whatever testimony of the senses they might appear to be substantiated. There is something truer, and more real, that what we can see with the eyes and touch with the finger. On such better evidence had Giovanni founded his confidence in Beatrice, though rather by the necessary force of her high attributes, than by any deep and generous faith on his part. But now his spirit was incapable of sustaining itself at the height to which the early enthusiasm of passion had exalted it; he fell down, groveling among earthly doubts, and defiled therewith the pure whiteness of Beatrice's image. Not that he gave her up; he did but distrust. He resolved to institute some decisive test that should satisfy him, once for all, whether there were those dreadful peculiarities in her physical nature which could not be supposed to exist without some corresponding monstrosity of soul. His eyes, gazing down afar, might have deceived him as to the insect and the flowers. But if he could witness, at the distance of a few paces, the sudden blight of one fresh and healthful flower in Beatrice's hand, there would be room for no further question. With this idea, he hastened to the florist and purchased a bouquet that was still gemmed with the morning dewdrops.

Before descending into the garden, Giovanni failed not to look at his figure in the mirror; a vanity to be expected in a beautiful young man, yet, as displaying itself at that troubled and feverish moment, the token of a certain shallowness of feeling and insincerity of character.

Recalling Facts

1. Giovanni had serious questions about
   - ☐ a. Beatrice's character.
   - ☐ b. Professor Baglioni's honesty.
   - ☐ c. Beatrice's true age.

2. In Beatrice's hand, a bouquet
   - ☐ a. was especially beautiful.
   - ☐ b. lost its attractions.
   - ☐ c. withered.

3. The insect perished after Beatrice
   - ☐ a. looked at it.
   - ☐ b. brushed at it.
   - ☐ c. breathed on it.

4. Giovanni was a
   - ☐ a. beautiful young man.
   - ☐ b. troubled mystic.
   - ☐ c. guileless and affectionate boy.

5. Giovanni wanted some freshly cut flowers in order to
   - ☐ a. test Beatrice.
   - ☐ b. impress Beatrice.
   - ☐ c. make peace with Beatrice.

Understanding the Passage

6. Giovanni appeared to be
   - ☐ a. in total agreement with Professor Baglioni.
   - ☐ b. confused and troubled by Beatrice.
   - ☐ c. fully aware of Beatrice's nature.

7. When Giovanni first saw Beatrice,
   - ☐ a. some strange things happened.
   - ☐ b. he was repulsed by her appearance.
   - ☐ c. he scarcely paid attention to her.

8. After a while, Giovanni
   - ☐ a. wanted to forget all about Beatrice.
   - ☐ b. began to deny what he had seen.
   - ☐ c. lost all his doubts about Beatrice.

9. Giovanni desperately needed
   - ☐ a. fresh flowers.
   - ☐ b. one more piece of evidence.
   - ☐ c. approval from Beatrice.

10. Before meeting Beatrice again, Giovanni
    - ☐ a. uncharacteristically lost his nerve.
    - ☐ b. began to feel a twinge of uncertainty.
    - ☐ c. decided to leave the flowers behind.

To General William Howe:

To argue with a man who has renounced the use and the authority of reason, and whose philosophy consists in holding humanity in contempt, is like administering medicine to the dead, or endeavoring to convert an atheist by scripture. Enjoy, sir, your insensibility of feeling and reflecting. It is the prerogative of animals. And no man will envy you these honors, in which a savage only can be your rival and a bear your master.

As the generosity of this country rewarded your brother's services last war, with an elegant monument in Westminster Abbey, it is consistent that she should bestow some mark of distinction upon you. You certainly deserve her notice, and a conspicuous place in the catalogue of extraordinary persons. Yet it would be a pity to pass you from the world in state, and consign you to magnificent oblivion among the tombs, without telling the future beholder why. Judas is as much known as John, yet history ascribes their fame to very different actions.

Sir William hath undoubtedly merited a monument; but of what kind, or with what inscription, where placed or how embellished, is a question that would puzzle all the heralds of St. James's in the profoundest mood of historical deliberation. We are at no loss, sir, to ascertain your real character, but somewhat perplexed how to perpetutate its identity, and preserve it uninjured from the transformations of time or mistake. A statuary may give a false expression to your bust, or decorate it with some equivocal emblems, by which you may happen to steal into reputation and impose upon the hereafter traditionary world. Ill-nature or ridicule may conspire, or a variety of accidents combine to lessen, enlarge, or change Sir William's fame; and no doubt but he who has taken so much pains to be singular in his conduct, would choose to be just as singular in his exit, his monument and his epitaph.

The usual honors of the dead, to be sure, are not sufficiently sublime to escort a character like you to the republic of dust and ashes; for however men may differ in their ideas of grandeur or of government here, the grave is nevertheless a perfect republic. The moment death obtains a conquest he loses a subject, and, like the foolish king you serve, will, in the end, war himself out of his dominions.

Recalling Facts

1. The country rewarded Howe's brother with a
   - ☐ a. monument.
   - ☐ b. seat in Parliament.
   - ☐ c. large pension.

2. Howe's brother was rewarded for his services during
   - ☐ a. an expedition.
   - ☐ b. a political crisis.
   - ☐ c. a war.

3. Judas was compared to
   - ☐ a. John.
   - ☐ b. William.
   - ☐ c. James.

4. The heralds were found at
   - ☐ a. Westminster Abbey.
   - ☐ b. St. James.
   - ☐ c. the graveyard.

5. The narrator considered Howe's king to be
   - ☐ a. wise.
   - ☐ b. perfect.
   - ☐ c. foolish.

Understanding the Passage

6. The narrator had a strong belief in the power of
   - ☐ a. reason.
   - ☐ b. faith.
   - ☐ c. tradition.

7. The narrator regarded highly the
   - ☐ a. concept of hereditary monarchy.
   - ☐ b. worth of all people.
   - ☐ c. things of nature.

8. The narrator regarded Howe
   - ☐ a. with contempt.
   - ☐ b. with affection.
   - ☐ c. as a misunderstood hero.

9. The narrator was most concerned about how future generations viewed
   - ☐ a. Howe.
   - ☐ b. himself.
   - ☐ c. St. James.

10. "The republic of dust and ashes" refers to the
    - ☐ a. failure of democratic governments.
    - ☐ b. equality of the grave.
    - ☐ c. King's rule over his dominions.

On the 20th of August, 1672, the city of the Hague, whose streets were ordinarily so neat and trim, and withal so tranquil that every day seemed like Sunday; the city of the Hague, with its shady park, its noble trees reaching out over the roofs of the Gothic dwelling, and its broad canals so calm and smooth that they resembled mammoth mirrors, wherein were reflected its myriad of church towers, whose graceful shapes recalled some city of the Orient—the city of the Hague, the capital of the Seven United Provinces, saw all its arteries swollen to bursting with a black and ● red flood of impetuous, breathless, eager citizens, who with knives in their belts, muskets on their shoulders, or clubs in their hands, were hurrying on toward the Buytenhof, a redoubtable prison, whose grated windows still frown on the beholder, where Cornelius de Witt, brother of the former Grand Pensionary of Holland, was languishing in confinement, on a charge of attempted murder preferred against him by the surgeon Tyckelaer.

If the history of that time—and especially of the year in the middle of which our narrative commences—were not indissolubly connected with the two names just mentioned, the few explanatory pages which follow might ● seem quite supererogatory; but we must first warn our dear friend, the indulgent reader, that this explanation is as indispensable to the right understanding of our tale as to that of the great event itself on which it is based.

Cornelius de Witt, Ruart de Pulten—that is to say, Inspector of Canals— ex-burgomaster of Dort, his native town, and member of the Assembly of the States of Holland, was forty-nine years of age when the Dutch people, weary of the Republic as it was administered by John de Witt, the Grand ● Pensionary of Holland, suddenly conceived a most violent affection for the Stadholderate, which had been abolished forever in Holland by the Perpetual Edict forced by John de Witt upon the United Provinces.

In accordance with the common experience that public opinion in its capricious flights seeks always to identify a principle with some man whose name is connected with its promulgation, the people saw the personification of the Republic in the stern features of the brothers De Witt, who disdained to pander to the whims of the mob, but were the unyielding upholders of liberty without license and prosperity without extravagance.

Recalling Facts

1. Ordinarily the streets of the Hague were
   - ☐ a. bustling.
   - ☐ b. tranquil.
   - ☐ c. violent.

2. The Hague's many church towers were reflected in its
   - ☐ a. small lakes.
   - ☐ b. narrow rivers.
   - ☐ c. broad canals.

3. Cornelius de Witt was in prison on the charge of
   - ☐ a. murder.
   - ☐ b. manslaughter.
   - ☐ c. attempted murder.

4. Cornelius de Witt grew up in the town of
   - ☐ a. Dort.
   - ☐ b. Buytenhof.
   - ☐ c. Pulten.

5. The brothers De Witt believed strongly in
   - ☐ a. the Stadholderate.
   - ☐ b. liberty without license.
   - ☐ c. prosperity to the point of extravagance.

Understanding the Passage

6. The street scene in The Hague was
   - ☐ a. most unusual.
   - ☐ b. threatening.
   - ☐ c. both a and b.

7. The narrator felt that the reader
   - ☐ a. should be impatient with details.
   - ☐ b. would be familiar with Tyckelaer.
   - ☐ c. needed this background information.

8. The people of the United Provinces
   - ☐ a. grew weary of the brothers De Witt.
   - ☐ b. were willing to die for the Republic.
   - ☐ c. both a and b.

9. The Stadholderate was
   - ☐ a. violently rejected by the people.
   - ☐ b. suddenly embraced by the people.
   - ☐ c. forgotten after it was abolished.

10. According to the narrator, people always
    - ☐ a. need to blame a specific individual.
    - ☐ b. hated the principles under lying the Republic.
    - ☐ c. preferred license to liberty.

Mrs. Dashwood remained at Norland several months; not from any disinclination to move when the sight of every well-known spot ceased to raise the violent emotion which it produced for a while; for when her spirits began to revive, and her mind became capable of some other exertion than that of heightening its affliction by melancholy remembrances, she was impatient to be gone, and indefatigable in her inquiries for a suitable dwelling in the neighborhood of Norland; for to remove far from that beloved spot was impossible. But she could hear of no situation that at once answered her notions of comfort and ease, and suited the prudence ● of her eldest daughter, whose steadier judgment rejected several houses as too large for their income, which her mother would have approved.

Mrs. Dashwood had been informed by her husband of the solemn promise on the part of his son in their favor, which gave comfort to his last earthly reflections. She doubted the sincerity of this assurance no more than he had doubted it himself, and she thought of it for her daughters' sake with satisfaction, though, as for herself, she was persuaded that a much smaller provision than seven thousand pounds would support ● her in affluence. For their brother's sake too, for the sake of his own heart, she rejoiced; and she reproached herself for being unjust to his merit before, in believing him incapable of generosity. His attentive behavior to herself and his sisters, convinced her that their welfare was dear to him, and, for a long time, she firmly relied on the liberality of his intentions.

The contempt which she had, very early in their acquaintance, felt for her daughter-in-law was very much increased by the further knowledge of her character, which half a year's residence in her family afforded; and, ● perhaps, in spite of every consideration of politeness or maternal affection on the side of the former, the two ladies might have found it impossible to have lived together so long, had not a particular circumstance occurred to give still greater eligibility, according to Mrs. Dashwood, to her daughters' continuance at Norland.

This circumstance was a growing attachment between her eldest girl and the brother of Mrs. John Dashwood, a gentlemanlike and pleasing young man, who was introduced to their acquaintance soon after his sister's establishment at Norland, and who had since spent the greatest part of his time there.

Recalling Facts

1. Mrs. Dashwood's mood was one of
   ☐ a. impatience.
   ☐ b. jubilation.
   ☐ c. quiet resignation.

2. Mrs. Dashwood wanted to find a place to live near
   ☐ a. the ocean.
   ☐ b. her father-in-law.
   ☐ c. Norland.

3. Mrs. Dashwood had been promised 7,000 pounds by her
   ☐ a. husband's son.
   ☐ b. husband.
   ☐ c. daughter-in-law.

4. Mrs. Dashwood had nothing but contempt for her
   ☐ a. brother.
   ☐ b. daughter-in-law.
   ☐ c. late husband.

5. Mrs. John Dashwood's brother
   ☐ a. rarely visited Norland.
   ☐ b. was crude and ill-mannered.
   ☐ c. spent most of his time at his sister's home.

Understanding the Passage

6. Mrs. Dashwood had recently been
   ☐ a. depressed.
   ☐ b. removed from her home.
   ☐ c. inconsolable.

7. Mrs. Dashwood had a hard time finding
   ☐ a. a decent doctor.
   ☐ b. a suitable house.
   ☐ c. an area of the country she liked.

8. Mrs. Dashwood's eldest daughter was
   ☐ a. happily married.
   ☐ b. constantly bickering with her mother.
   ☐ c. careful about money.

9. Mrs. Dashwood had recently lived with
   ☐ a. her daughter-in-law's family.
   ☐ b. two elderly lady friends.
   ☐ c. her mother and father.

10. The eldest daughter
    ☐ a. might soon get married.
    ☐ b. needed money for acceptance into society.
    ☐ c. rejected the advances of a young gentleman.

Much was said and written, at the time, concerning the policy of adding the vast regions of Louisiana to the already immense and but half-tenanted territories of the United States. As the warmth of controversy, however, subsided, and party considerations gave place to more liberal views, the wisdom of the measure began to be generally conceded. It soon became apparent to the meanest capacity, that while nature had placed a barrier of desert to the extension of our population in the West, the measure had made us the masters of a belt of fertile country, which, in the revolutions of the day, might have become the property of a rival nation. It gave us the sole command of the great thoroughfare of the interior, and placed the countless tribes of Indians, who lay along our borders, entirely within our control; it reconciled conflicting rights, and quieted national distrusts; it opened a thousand avenues to the inland trade, and to the waters of the Pacific; and, if ever time or necessity shall require a peaceful division of this vast empire, it assures us of a neighbor that will possess our language, our religion, our institutions, and, it is also to be hoped, our sense of political justice.

Although the purchase was made in 1803, the spring of the succeeding year was permitted to open, before the official prudence of the Spaniard, who held the province for his European master, admitted the authority, or even the entrance of its new proprietors. But the forms of the transfer were no sooner completed, and the new government acknowledged, than swarms of that restless people which is ever found hovering on the skirts of American society, plunged into the thickets that fringed the right bank of the Mississippi, with the same careless hardihood that had already sustained so many of them in their toilsome progress from the Atlantic States, the eastern shores of the "Father of Rivers."

Time was necessary to blend the numerous and affluent colonists of the lower province with their new compatriots: but the thinner and more humble population above was almost immediately swallowed in the vortex which attended the tide of instant emigration. The inroad from the East was a new and sudden outbreaking of a people who had endured a momentary restraint, after having been rendered nearly resistless by success. The toils and hazards of former undertakings were forgotten.

Recalling Facts

1. The purchase of Louisiana
   - ☐ a. prevented a rival nation from controlling it.
   - ☐ b. was quickly applauded by all Americans.
   - ☐ c. both a and b.

2. The barrier to western expansion was believed to be
   - ☐ a. a mountain range.
   - ☐ b. a desert.
   - ☐ c. hostile European powers.

3. The Spanish did not withdraw until the spring of
   - ☐ a. 1802.
   - ☐ b. 1803.
   - ☐ c. 1804.

4. When the new government was acknowledged, Americans
   - ☐ a. flocked to the Mississippi.
   - ☐ b. slowly made plans to move west.
   - ☐ c. tried to drive foreigners out.

5. The tide of emigration came from the
   - ☐ a. South.
   - ☐ b. West.
   - ☐ c. East.

Understanding the Passage

6. At first, those who supported the purchase of Louisiana were considered
   - ☐ a. reactionaries.
   - ☐ b. conservatives.
   - ☐ c. liberals.

7. The narrator saw the purchase of Louisiana as
   - ☐ a. something unproductive
   - ☐ b. a mixed blessing.
   - ☐ c. a fantastic opportunity.

8. The "Father of Rivers" was another term for the
   - ☐ a. Great American Desert.
   - ☐ b. Mississippi River.
   - ☐ c. Eastern seacoast.

9. The primary motive for the new emigrants was
   - ☐ a. money.
   - ☐ b. land.
   - ☐ c. power.

10. The people who moved west did so
    - ☐ a. reluctantly.
    - ☐ b. eagerly.
    - ☐ c. cautiously.

It is a trite but true observation that examples work more forcibly than precepts: and if this be just in what is odious and blameable, it is more strongly so in what is amiable and praiseworthy. Here emulation most effectually operates upon us, and inspires our imitation in an irresistable manner. A good man therefore is a standing lesson to all his acquaintances, and of far greater use in that narrow circle than a good book.

But as it often happens that the best men are unknown, and consequently cannot extend the usefulness of their examples; the writer may be called to spread their history farther, and to present the amiable pictures to those who have not the happiness of knowing the originals; and so, by communicating such valuable patterns to the world, he may perhaps do a more extensive service to mankind than the person whose life originally afforded the pattern.

In this light I have always regarded those biographers who have recorded the actions of great and worthy persons of both sexes. Not to mention those ancient writers which of late days are little read, being written in obsolete, and as they are generally thought, unintelligible languages, such as Plutarch, Nepos, and others which I heard of in my youth; our own language affords many of excellent use and instruction, finely calculated to sow the seeds of virtue in youth, and very easy to be comprehended by persons of moderate capacity. Such as the history of John the Great, who, by his brave and heroic actions against men of large and athletic bodies, obtained the glorious appellation of the Giant Killer; that of an Earl of Warwick, whose Christian name was Guy; the lives of Argalus and Parthenia; and above all, the history of those seven worthy personages, the Champions of Christendom. In all these delight is mixed with instruction, and the reader is almost as much improved as entertained.

But I pass by these and many others to mention two books lately published, which represent an admirable pattern of the amiable in either sex. The former of these, which deals in male virtue, was written by the great person himself, who lived the life he hath recorded, and is thought by many to have lived such a life only in order to write it; the other is communicated to us by an historian who borrows his lights from authentic papers and records.

Recalling Facts

1. The narrator believes that examples work best when they involve the
   - ☐ a. odious and blameable.
   - ☐ b. oblique and devious.
   - ☐ c. amiable and praiseworthy.

2. According to the narrator, a good man who is unknown needs the services of a
   - ☐ a. lawyer.
   - ☐ b. writer.
   - ☐ c. physician.

3. Plutarch was a
   - ☐ a. neglected ancient writer.
   - ☐ b. great military leader.
   - ☐ c. widely read biographer.

4. John the Great was known as
   - ☐ a. the Giant Killer.
   - ☐ b. the Earl of Warwick.
   - ☐ c. a Champion of Christendom.

5. The narrator is about to inform the reader about
   - ☐ a. his own life.
   - ☐ b. two books recently published.
   - ☐ c. the lives of the Champions of Christendom.

Understanding the Passage

6. The narrator has the highest praise for good
   - ☐ a. ideas.
   - ☐ b. people.
   - ☐ c. books.

7. A noble profession, according to the narrator, is
   - ☐ a. writing poetry.
   - ☐ b. writing biographies.
   - ☐ c. practicing law.

8. The narrator does not exclude the importance of
   - ☐ a. good women.
   - ☐ b. writers in obsolete languages.
   - ☐ c. both a and b.

9. The narrator feels that the best books in his language are understandable
   - ☐ a. only to literate adults.
   - ☐ b. only to well-educated professionals.
   - ☐ c. to the young and the moderately intelligent.

10. The first recently published book the narrator recommends is
    - ☐ a. an autobiography.
    - ☐ b. a biography.
    - ☐ c. a book of old sayings.

To avoid mistake, I would say that I not only commend the study of literature but wish our sources of supply and comparison vastly enlarged. American students may well derive from all former lands—from forenoon Greece and Rome, down to the perturbed medieval times, the Crusades, and so to Italy, the German intellect—all the older literatures, and all the newer ones—from witty and warlike France, and markedly and in many ways and at many different periods, from the enterprise and soul of the great Spanish race—bearing ourselves always courteous, always deferential, indebted beyond measure to the mother-world, to all its nations dead, as all its nations living—the offspring, this America of ours, the daughter, not by any means of the British isles exclusively but of the continent, and all continents. Indeed, it is time we should realize and fully fructify those germs we also hold from Italy, France, Spain, especially in the best imaginative productions of those lands, which are in many ways loftier and subtler than the English, or British, and indispensable to complete our service, proportions, education, reminiscences, *etc.* The British element these States hold, and have always held, enormously beyond its fit proportions. I have already spoken of Shakespeare. He seems to me of astral genius, first class, entirely fit for feudalism. His contributions, especially to the literature of the passions, are immense, forever dear to humanity—and his name is always to be reverenced in America. But there is much in him ever offensive to democracy. He is not only the tally of feudalism, but I should say Shakespeare is incarnated, uncompromising feudalism, in literature.

I add that—while England is among the greatest of lands in political freedom, or the idea of it, and in stalwart personal character—the spirit of English literature is not great, at least is not greatest—and its products are no models for us. With the exception of Shakespeare, there is no first-class genius in that literature—which, with a truly vast amount of value, and of artificial beauty, is almost always material, sensual, not spiritual—almost always congests, makes plethoric, not frees, expands, dilates—is cold, antidemocratic, loves to be sluggish and stately, and shows much of that characteristic of vulgar persons, the dread of saying or doing something not at all improper in itself, but unconventional, and that may be laughed at.

Recalling Facts

1. The narrator referred to medieval times as
   - ☐ a. witty.
   - ☐ b. perturbed.
   - ☐ c. golden.

2. The "daughter" in this passage is
   - ☐ a. America.
   - ☐ b. the Spanish race.
   - ☐ c. the older literatures.

3. The narrator praised
   - ☐ a. British literature in general.
   - ☐ b. Italian and Spanish literature.
   - ☐ c. feudalism.

4. According to the narrator, Shakespeare was not a friend of
   - ☐ a. humanity.
   - ☐ b. feudalism.
   - ☐ c. democracy.

5. As a land of great political freedom, the narrator singled out
   - ☐ a. Italy.
   - ☐ b. Greece.
   - ☐ c. England.

Understanding the Passage

6. The term "mother-world" refers to
   - ☐ a. America's unusually large land mass.
   - ☐ b. the British isles exclusively.
   - ☐ c. the European nations responsible for a cultural legacy.

7. The narrator maintained that Americans should feel
   - ☐ a. extremely grateful.
   - ☐ b. defiant.
   - ☐ c. culturally inferior.

8. The narrator suggested that Americans should rely less on
   - ☐ a. British literature.
   - ☐ b. French literature.
   - ☐ c. Spanish literature.

9. For literary models, the narrator advised Americans to
   - ☐ a. study Shakespeare first.
   - ☐ b. rely on Greek classics.
   - ☐ c. not rely on English writers.

10. According to the narrator, English literature
    - ☐ a. lacks warmth and human feeling.
    - ☐ b. should be generally ignored.
    - ☐ c. is often lively and unconventional.

33 *from* The Autobiography of Benjamin Franklin

I had been religiously educated as a Presbyterian; and tho' some of the dogmas of the persuasion, such as the eternal decrees of God, election, reprobation, etc., appeared to me unintelligible, others doubtful, and I early absented myself from the public assemblies of the sect, Sunday being my studying day, I never was without some religious principles. I never doubted, for instance, the existence of the Deity, that he made the world and governed it by his providence, that the most acceptable service of God was the doing good to man, that our souls are all immortal, and that all crime will be punished and virtue rewarded either here or hereafter. These I esteemed the essentials of every religion, and being to be found in all the religions we had in our country, I respected them all, tho' with different degrees of respect as I found them more or less mixed with other articles which without any tendency to inspire, promote, or confirm morality, served principally to divide us and make us unfriendly to one another. This respect to all, with an opinion that the worst had some good effects, induced me to avoid all discourse that might tend to lessen the good opinion another might have of his own religion; and as our province increased in people and new places of worship were continually wanted and generally erected by voluntary contribution, my mite for such purpose, whatever might be the sect, was never refused.

Tho' I seldom attended any public worship, I had still an opinion of its propriety and of its utility when rightly conducted, and I regularly paid my annual subscription for the support of the only Presbyterian minister or meeting we had in Philadelphia. He used to visit me sometimes as a friend and admonish me to attend his administrations, and I was now and then prevailed on to do so, once for five Sundays successively. Had he been, in my opinion, a good preacher, perhaps I might have continued, notwithstanding the occasion I had for the Sunday's leisure in my course of study; but his discourses were chiefly either polemic arguments or explications of the peculiar doctrines of our sect, and were all to me very dry, uninteresting, and unedifying since not a single moral principle was inculcated or enforced, their aim seemingly to be rather to make us Presbyterians than good citizens.

Recalling Facts

1. The narrator believed that certain Presbyterian dogmas were
   - ☐ a. essential.
   - ☐ b. unintelligible.
   - ☐ c. slightly flawed.

2. On Sundays, the narrator usually
   - ☐ a. studied.
   - ☐ b. went to church.
   - ☐ c. gave lectures.

3. The narrator thought that the best service to God was
   - ☐ a. praying.
   - ☐ b. supporting the church.
   - ☐ c. helping other people.

4. The narrator tried to avoid arguments over
   - ☐ a. politics.
   - ☐ b. economics.
   - ☐ c. religion.

5. The narrator found his minister's sermons
   - ☐ a. unedifying.
   - ☐ b. interesting.
   - ☐ c. rousing.

Understanding the Passage

6. To the narrator, attending church was
   - ☐ a. an important part of being a Christian.
   - ☐ b. not as important as his other Sunday activities.
   - ☐ c. the only way to learn basic moral principles.

7. The narrator felt that most religions
   - ☐ a. shared certain basic elements.
   - ☐ b. were disruptive to society.
   - ☐ c. lacked a distinct hierarchy of worshippers.

8. The narrator tried not to
   - ☐ a. insult people who belonged to different religions.
   - ☐ b. differentiate between moral and immoral behavior.
   - ☐ c. miss his minister's Sunday sermons.

9. The narrator supported the Presbyterian church with his
   - ☐ a. labor.
   - ☐ b. money.
   - ☐ c. preaching.

10. The narrator didn't like those elements of a religion which
    - ☐ a. promoted the notion of an afterlife.
    - ☐ b. turned people against each other.
    - ☐ c. both a and b.

from **The Old Wives' Tales** *by Arnold Bennett*

It was during the month of June that Aunt Harriet came from Axe to spend a few days with her little sister, Mrs. Baines. The railway between Axe and the Five Towns had not yet been opened; but even if it had been opened Aunt Harriet would probably not have used it; she always traveled from Axe to Bursley in the same vehicle, a small wagonette which she hired from Bratt's livery stables at Axe, driven by a coachman who thoroughly understood the importance, and the peculiarities, of Aunt Harriet.

Mrs. Baines had increased in stoutness, so that now Aunt Harriet had very little advantage over her physically, but the moral ascendency of the elder still persisted. The two vast widows shared Mrs. Baines's bedroom, spending much of their time there in long, hushed conversations—interviews from which Mrs. Baines emerged with the air of one who has received enlightenment and Aunt Harriet with the air of one who has rendered it. The pair went about together, in the shop, the showroom, the parlor, the kitchen, and also into the town, addressing each other as "Sister," "Sister"—everywhere it was "Sister," "Sister," "My dear sister." They referred to each other as oracular sources of wisdom and good taste. Respectability stalked abroad when they were afoot, and the whole square wriggled uneasily as though God's eye were peculiarly upon it. The meals in the parlor became solemn collations, at which shone the best silver and the finest linen, but from which gaiety and naturalness appeared to be banished. (I say "appeared" because it cannot be doubted that Aunt Harriet was natural, and there were moments when she possibly considered herself to be practicing gaiety—a gaiety more desolating than her severity.) The younger generation was extinguished, pressed flat and lifeless under the ponderosity of the widows.

Mr. Povey wasn't the man to be easily flattened by ponderosity of any kind, and his suppression was a striking example of the prowess of the widows; who, indeed, went over Mr. Povey like traction engines, with the sublime unconsciousness of traction engines, leaving an inanimate object in the road behind them, and scarce aware even of the jolt. Mr. Povey hated Aunt Harriet, but, lying crushed there in the road, how could he rebel? He felt that Aunt Harriet was constantly adding him up, and reporting the result at frequent intervals to Mrs. Baines in the bedroom.

Recalling Facts

1. Aunt Harriet always took a small wagonette from Axe to
   - ☐ a. Bursley.
   - ☐ b. Poveytown.
   - ☐ c. Brattleboro.

2. Mrs. Baines had recently
   - ☐ a. lost weight.
   - ☐ b. married her second husband.
   - ☐ c. neither a nor b.

3. During Aunt Harriet's visit, she and Mrs. Baines
   - ☐ a. made each other uncomfortable.
   - ☐ b. spent most of their time together.
   - ☐ c. felt like equals in all respects.

4. The younger generation felt overwhelmed by the widows'
   - ☐ a. intelligence.
   - ☐ b. ponderosity.
   - ☐ c. gaiety.

5. Mr. Povey hated
   - ☐ a. Mrs. Baines.
   - ☐ b. Aunt Harriet.
   - ☐ c. his own lack of confidence.

Understanding the Passage

6. When Aunt Harriet traveled, she was
   - ☐ a. willing to be adventurous.
   - ☐ b. always uncomfortable.
   - ☐ c. a creature of habit.

7. Apparently, Aunt Harriet was
   - ☐ a. physically large.
   - ☐ b. tolerant of people's differences.
   - ☐ c. the life of the party.

8. The one thing that separated Aunt Harriet and Mrs. Baines was Aunt Harriet's
   - ☐ a. personal wealth.
   - ☐ b. physical attractiveness.
   - ☐ c. moral superiority.

9. Aunt Harriet and Mrs. Baines
   - ☐ a. intimidated other people
   - ☐ b. were great storytellers.
   - ☐ c. were praised by others for their wisdom and good taste.

10. Mr. Povey was apparently
    - ☐ a. a close friend of the widows.
    - ☐ b. no match for the widows
    - ☐ c. a road engineer for the town.

Thessalonica, in consequence of its commercial situation, was populous and rich. Its fortifications and numerous garrison had preserved it from injury during the late commotions, and the number of inhabitants was greatly increased, at the expense of the defenseless districts and cities. Its place, with relation to Dalmatia, the Peloponnesus, and the Danube, was nearly centrical. Its security had been uninterrupted for ages, and no city in the empire of Theodosius exhibited so many monuments of its ancient prosperity. It had been, for many years, the residence of the prince, and had thence become the object of a kind of filial affection. He had labored to render it impregnable, by erecting bulwarks, and guarding it with the bravest of his troops; he had endowed the citizens with new revenues and privileges, had enhanced the frequency of their shows, and the magnificence of their halls and avenues, and made it the seat of government of Illyria and Greece.

Its defense was entrusted to Botheric, whom he had selected for his valor, fidelity, and moderation; and he commended, with equal zeal to this officer, the defense of the city from external enemies, and the maintenance of justice and order within its walls.

The temper of Botheric was generous and impetuous. He was unacquainted with civil forms, and refrained, as much as possible, from encroaching on the functions of the magistrate. His education and genius were military, and he conceived that his commission required from him nothing but unwearied attention to his soldiers. His vigilance was bent to maintain order and obedience among them, and to prevent or to stifle dissentions between them and the citizens. For this end he multiplied their duties and exercises—their time was constantly occupied with attendance at their stations, or performance of some personal duty in their quarters.

By these means the empire of order was, for some time, maintained; but no diligence or moderation can fully restrain the passions of the multitude. You need not be told that the populace of Roman cities are actuated by a boundless passion for public shows. Quarrels sometimes arose between the spectators at the theater and circus, and the sentinels who were planted in the avenues. The general was always present at the public shows; clamor and riot instantly attracted his attention, and if a soldier was a party in the fray he hasted to terminate the contest by examination and punishment.

Recalling Facts

1. Thessalonica's population had
   - ☐ a. declined in recent years.
   - ☐ b. remained fairly stable.
   - ☐ c. grown rapidly.

2. Thessalonica was located in
   - ☐ a. the empire of Botheric.
   - ☐ b. the empire of Theodosius.
   - ☐ c. Dalmatia.

3. The seat of government of Illyria and Greece was at
   - ☐ a. Thessalonica.
   - ☐ b. Dalmatia.
   - ☐ c. Rome.

4. Botheric's education was in
   - ☐ a. the fine arts.
   - ☐ b. military affairs.
   - ☐ c. engineering.

5. The people in Roman cities had a great passion for
   - ☐ a. private parties.
   - ☐ b. public shows.
   - ☐ c. their military protectors.

Understanding the Passage

6. Thessalonica apparently needed
   - ☐ a. more people.
   - ☐ b. strong military protection
   - ☐ c. a more conscientious leader.

7. Compared to other cities, Thessalonica was
   - ☐ a. in poor condition.
   - ☐ b. still great, but fading slowly.
   - ☐ c. in an enviable position.

8. Botheric appeared to be
   - ☐ a. miserable in his position.
   - ☐ b. poorly trained for his position.
   - ☐ c. generally well qualified for his position.

9. Botheric tried to make sure that his soldiers had
   - ☐ a. a great deal of work to do.
   - ☐ b. lots of free time.
   - ☐ c. no contact with civilians.

10. Relations between the citizens and the soldiers were
    - ☐ a. peaceful and cooperative.
    - ☐ b. endangering the empire.
    - ☐ c. strained and rather delicate.

Webster well deserves to be called the Defender of the Constitution. His leaders are the men of 1787. "I have never made an effort," he says, "and never propose to make an effort; I have never countenanced an effort, and never mean to countenance an effort, to disturb the arrangement as originally made, by which the various States came into the Union." Still thinking of the sanction which the Constitution gives to slavery, he says, "Because it was a part of the original compact, let it stand." Notwithstanding his special acuteness and ability, he is unable to take a fact out of its merely political relations, and behold it as it lies absolutely to be disposed of by the intellect—what, for instance, it behooves a man to do here in America today with regard to slavery—but ventures to make some such desperate answer as the following, while professing to speak absolutely, and as a private man—from which what new and singular code of social duties might be inferred? "The manner," says he, "in which the governments of those States where slavery exists are to regulate it is for their own consideration, under their responsibility to their constituents, to the general laws of propriety, humanity, and justice, and to God. Associations formed elsewhere, springing from a feeling of humanity, or other cause, have nothing whatever to do with it. They have never received any encouragement from me, and they never will."

They who know of no purer sources of truth, who have traced up its stream no higher, stand, and wisely stand, by the Bible and the Constitution, and drink at it there with reverence and humility; but they who behold where it comes trickling into this lake or that pool, gird up their loins once more, and continue their pilgrimage toward its fountainhead.

No man with a genius for legislation has appeared in America; they are rare in the history of the world. There are orators, politicians, and eloquent men, by the thousand; but the speaker has not yet opened his mouth to speak who is capable of settling the much-vexed questions of the day. Our legislators have not yet learned the comparative value of free trade and of freedom, of union, and of rectitude, to a nation. They have no genius or talent for comparatively humble questions of taxation and finance, commerce and manufactures and agriculture.

Recalling Facts

1. Webster's leaders were the men of
   - ☐ a. 1620.
   - ☐ b. 1776.
   - ☐ c. 1787.

2. Webster wanted the Constitution's language about slavery to
   - ☐ a. stay the same.
   - ☐ b. be dropped.
   - ☐ c. be modified.

3. Webster felt that the issue of slavery should be dealt with by
   - ☐ a. the state governments where slavery existed.
   - ☐ b. each person as an individual.
   - ☐ c. the national Congress.

4. The narrator said that America has produced no one with a genius for
   - ☐ a. legislation.
   - ☐ b. exploration.
   - ☐ c. political relations.

5. One of the great questions of the day mentioned by the narrator was
   - ☐ a. voting rights.
   - ☐ b. free trade.
   - ☐ c. balance of payments.

Understanding the Passage

6. The original Constitution
   - ☐ a. condemned slavery.
   - ☐ b. approved slavery.
   - ☐ c. failed to mention slavery.

7. The narrator felt that Webster's defense of slavery was
   - ☐ a. worthless.
   - ☐ b. of some value.
   - ☐ c. a moral guide for all to follow.

8. The narrator felt that the highest source of truth was
   - ☐ a. the Bible.
   - ☐ b. the Constitution.
   - ☐ c. neither a nor b.

9. According to the narrator, the fountainhead of truth is
   - ☐ a. worth striving for even if it will never be reached.
   - ☐ b. beyond the bible and the Constitution.
   - ☐ c. both a and b.

10. According to the narrator, the legislators of his day did
    - ☐ a. an excellent job.
    - ☐ b. a fair job.
    - ☐ c. a poor job.

Miss Dorothea Brooke was usually spoken of as being remarkably clever, but with the addition that her sister Celia had more common sense. Nevertheless, Celia wore scarcely more trimmings; and it was only to close observers that her dress differed from her sister's, and had a shade of coquetry in its arrangements; for Dorothea Brooke's plain dressing was due to mixed conditions, in most of which her sister shared. The pride of being ladies had something to do with it: the Brooke connections, though not exactly aristocratic, were unquestionably "good": if you inquired backward for a generation or two, you would not find any yard-measuring or parcel-tying forefathers—anything lower than an admiral or a clergyman; and there was even an ancestor discernible as a Puritan gentleman who served under Cromwell, but afterwards conformed, and managed to come out of all political troubles as the proprietor of a respectable family estate. Young women of such birth, living in a quiet country house, and attending a village church hardly larger than a parlor, naturally regarded frippery as the ambition of a huckster's daughter. Then there was well-bred economy, which in those days made show in dress the first item to be deducted from, when any margin was required for expenses more distinctive of rank. Such reasons would have been enough to account for plain dress, quite apart from religious feeling; but in Dorothea Brooke's case, religion alone would have determined it; and Celia mildly acquiesced in all her sister's sentiments, only infusing them with that common sense which is able to accept momentous doctrines without any eccentric agitation. Dorothea knew many passages of Pascal's *Penseés* and of Jeremy Taylor by heart; and to her the destinies of mankind, seen by the light of Christianity, made the solicitudes of feminine fashion appear an occupation for Bedlam. She could not reconcile the anxieties of a spiritual life involving eternal consequences, with a keen interest in guimpe and artificial protrusions of drapery. Her mind was theoretic, and yearned by its nature after some lofty conception of the world which might frankly include the parish of Tipton and her own rule of conduct there; she was enamoured of intensity and greatness, and rash in embracing whatever seemed to her to have those aspects; likely to seek martyrdom, to make retractations, and then to incur martyrdom after all in a quarter where she had not sought it.

Recalling Facts

1. People usually thought of Dorothea Brooke as
   - ☐ a. hopelessly old-fashioned.
   - ☐ b. remarkably clever.
   - ☐ c. completely self-centered.

2. Dorothea Brooke came from
   - ☐ a. a disgraced family.
   - ☐ b. an aristocratic family.
   - ☐ c. a good family.

3. One of Dorothea's ancestors had been a
   - ☐ a. yard measurer.
   - ☐ b. Puritan gentleman.
   - ☐ c. convicted felon.

4. Celia had
   - ☐ a. no religious feelings.
   - ☐ b. more common sense than her sister.
   - ☐ c. memorized many passages of Pascal's Penseés.

5. The Brooke sisters lived
   - ☐ a. in the country.
   - ☐ b. with their grandmother.
   - ☐ c. both a and b.

Understanding the Passage

6. The Brooke sisters felt that fancy clothes were
   - ☐ a. not a necessity.
   - ☐ b. the best measure of a person's worth.
   - ☐ c. never to be worn on weekdays.

7. Dorothea and Celia both had
   - ☐ a. a fair amount of pride.
   - ☐ b. husbands and small children to care for.
   - ☐ c. a loathing for manual labor.

8. Dorothea searched for
   - ☐ a. a larger meaning in her world.
   - ☐ b. her father's hidden letters
   - ☐ c. a chance to break away from Celia's control.

9. Celia accepted religion
   - ☐ a. without any excessive questioning.
   - ☐ b. only after her sister's prodding.
   - ☐ c. as an excuse not to marry.

10. Dorothea was attracted to
    - ☐ a. the local clergyman.
    - ☐ b. things which had the appearance of greatness.
    - ☐ c. the doctrine of self-denial.

The habits of Basil Mertoun were retired and gloomy. From loud mirth he instantly fled; and even the moderated cheerfulness of a friendly party, had the invariable effect of throwing him into deeper dejection than even his usual demeanor indicated.

Women are always particularly desirous of investigating mystery, and of alleviating melancholy, especially when these circumstances are united in a handsome man about the prime of life. It is possible, therefore, that amongst the fair-haired and blue-eyed daughters of Thule this mysterious and pensive stranger might have found someone to take upon herself the task of consolation, had he shown any willingness to accept such kindly offices; but, far from doing so, he seemed even to shun the presence of the sex, to which in our distresses, whether of mind or body, we generally apply for pity and comfort.

To these peculiarities Mr. Mertoun added another, which was particularly disagreeable to his host and principal patron, Magnus Troil. This magnate of Zetland, descended by the father's side, as we have already said, from an ancient Norwegian family by the marriage of its representative with a Danish lady, held the devout opinion that a cup of Geneva or Nantz was specific against all cares and afflictions whatever. These were remedies to which Mr. Mertoun never applied; his drink was water, and water alone, and no persuasion or entreaties could induce him to taste any stronger beverage than was afforded by the pure stream. Now this Magnus Troil could not tolerate; it was a defiance to the ancient northern laws of conviviality, which, for his own part, he had so rigidly observed, that although he was wont to assert that he had never in his life gone to bed drunk (that is, in his own sense of the word), it would have been impossible to prove that he had ever resigned himself to slumber in a state of actual and absolute sobriety. It may be therefore asked, What did this stranger bring into society to compensate the displeasure given by his austere and abstemious habits? He had, in the first place, that manner and self-importance which mark a person of some consequence; and although it was conjectured that he could not be rich, yet it was certainly known by his expenditure that neither was he absolutely poor. He had, besides, some powers of conversation, when he chose to exert them.

Recalling Facts

1. Basil Mertoun routinely
   fled from
   □ a. laughter and gaiety.
   □ b. strangers and unknown
   objects.
   □ c. conversations centered
   around politics.

2. Basil Mertoun seemed
   to dislike
   □ a. nature.
   □ b. Zetland.
   □ c. women.

3. Magnus Troil was the
   principal patron of
   □ a. Basil Mertoun.
   □ b. ladies of Danish descent.
   □ c. daughters of Thule.

4. Basil Mertoun only drank
   □ a. Geneva.
   □ b. pure water.
   □ c. Irish coffee.

5. It was clear that Basil Mertoun
   was not
   □ a. handsome.
   □ b. quite intelligent.
   □ c. without some money.

Understanding the Passage

6. The narrator believed that
   women did not flock around
   Basil Mertoun simply
   because he
   □ a. gave them no
   encouragement.
   □ b. had no air of mystery
   about him.
   □ c. had not mastered the art
   of conversation.

7. Mr. Troil tried to get
   Mr. Mertoun to
   □ a. have a cup of Geneva.
   □ b. attend his exclusive parties
   □ c. become a misanthrope.

8. Mr. Troil was apparently
   □ a. stingy with his money.
   □ b. a man of austere habits.
   □ c. a regular drinker.

9. Mr. Troil believed that the
   laws of conviviality required
   Basil Mertoun to
   □ a. host the next party.
   □ b. have a drink of alcohol.
   □ c. pay more attention to
   the ladies.

10. Basil Mertoun could best be
    described as
    □ a. generous.
    □ b. reclusive.
    □ c. unprincipled.

Mrs. Lee soon became popular. Her parlor was a favorite haunt of certain men and women who had the art of finding its mistress at home; an art which seemed not to be within the powers of everybody. Old Baron Jacobi, the Bulgarian minister, fell madly in love with Madeleine Lee and her sister Sybil, as he commonly did with every pretty face and neat figure. He was a witty, cynical, broken-down Parisian rake, kept in Washington for years past by his debts and his salary; always grumbling because there was no opera, and mysteriously disappearing on visits to New York; a voracious devourer of French and German literature, especially of novels; a man who seemed to have met every noted or notorious personage of the century, and whose mind was a magazine of amusing information; an excellent musical critic, who was not afraid to criticize Sybil's singing; a connoisseur in bric-a-brac, who laughed at Madeleine's display of odds and ends, and occasionally brought her a Persian plate or a bit of embroidery, which he said was good and would do her credit. This old sinner believed in everything that was perverse and wicked, but he accepted the prejudices of Anglo-Saxon society, and was too clever to obtrude his opinions upon others. He would have married both sisters at once more willingly than either alone, but as he feelingly said, "If I were forty years younger, mademoiselle, you should not sing to me so calmly." His friend Popoff, an intelligent, vivacious Russian, with very Calmuck features and passionately fond of music, hung over Sybil's piano by the hour; he brought Russian airs which he taught her to sing.

A very different visitor was Mr. French, a young member of Congress from Connecticut, who aspired to act the part of the educated gentleman in politics, and to purify the public tone. He had reform principles and an unfortunately conceited manner; he was rather wealthy, rather clever, rather well educated, rather honest, and rather vulgar. His allegiance was divided between Mrs. Lee and her sister, whom he infuriated by addressing as "Miss Sybil" with patronizing familiarity. He was particularly strong in what he called "badinaige," and his playful but ungainly attempts at wit drove Mrs. Lee beyond the bounds of patience; but still he was useful, always bubbling with the latest political gossip, and deeply interested in the fate of party stakes.

Recalling Facts

1. Old Baron Jacobi was a
   minister from
   ☐ a. Bulgaria.
   ☐ b. Romania.
   ☐ c. Armenia.

2. Jacobi had been
   in Washington
   ☐ a. only a few days.
   ☐ b. several months.
   ☐ c. several years.

3. Jacobi was not afraid to
   criticize Sybil's
   ☐ a. painting.
   ☐ b. singing.
   ☐ c. writing.

4. Popoff was passionately
   fond of
   ☐ a. dancing.
   ☐ b. music.
   ☐ c. poetry.

5. Politically, Mr. French
   considered himself a
   ☐ a. reformer.
   ☐ b. conservative.
   ☐ c. revolutionary.

Understanding the Passage

6. Madeleine and Sybil were
   ☐ a. sisters.
   ☐ b. friends.
   ☐ c. mother and daughter.

7. While in New York, Jacobi
   probably went to the
   ☐ a. museum.
   ☐ b. opera.
   ☐ c. library.

8. Jacobi could best be
   described as
   ☐ a. a boring, listless
      old man.
   ☐ b. a man of the world.
   ☐ c. highly sensitive and
      easily hurt.

9. Jacobi was a man with
   ☐ a. strong Anglo-Saxon
      prejudices.
   ☐ b. narrow interests.
   ☐ c. strong passions.

10. Mr. French thought very
    highly of
    ☐ a. Sybil.
    ☐ b. Popoff.
    ☐ c. himself.

It makes me melancholy to see how like fools some very sensible people act in the matter of choosing wives. They perplex their judgments by a most undue attention to little niceties of personal appearances, habits, disposition, and other trifles which concern nobody but the lady herself. An unhappy gentleman resolving to wed nothing short of perfection keeps his heart and hand till both get so old and withered that no tolerable woman will accept them. Now, this is the very height of absurdity. A kind Providence has so skillfully adapted sex to sex and the mass of individuals ● to each other that, with certain obvious exceptions, any male and female may be moderately happy in the married state. The true rule is to ascertain that the match is fundamentally a good one, and then to take it for granted that all minor objections, should there be such, will vanish if you let them alone. Only put yourself beyond hazard as to the real basis of matrimonial bliss, and it is scarcely to be imagined what miracles in the way of reconciling smaller incongruities connubial love will effect.

For my own part, I freely confess that in my bachelorship I was precisely ● such an over-curious simpleton as I now advise the reader not to be. My early habits had gifted me with a feminine sensibility and too exquisite refinement. I was the accomplished graduate of a dry goods store where by dint of ministering to the whims of the fine ladies, and suiting silken hose to delicate limbs, and handling satins, ribbons, chintzes, calicoes, tapes, gauze, and cambric needles, I grew up a very ladylike sort of a gentleman. It is not assuming too much to affirm that the ladies themselves were hardly so ladylike as Thomas Bullfrog. So painfully acute was my sense ● of female imperfection, and such varied excellence did I require in the woman whom I could love, that there was an awful risk of my getting no wife at all or of being driven to perpetrate matrimony with my own image in the looking glass. Besides the fundamental principle already hinted at, I demanded the fresh bloom of youth, pearly teeth, glossy ringlets, and the whole list of lovely items, with the utmost delicacy of habits and sentiments, a silken texture of mind, and, above all, a virgin heart—in a word, a young angel just from Paradise.

Recalling Facts

1. The narrator laments the fact that many men want their wives to be
   - □ a. kind.
   - □ b. healthy.
   - □ c. perfect.

2. The narrator thinks that most married couples can
   - □ a. be blissfully happy.
   - □ b. be moderately happy.
   - □ c. never be happy.

3. The narrator once worked in a
   - □ a. hardware store.
   - □ b. dry goods store.
   - □ c. grocery store.

4. Thomas Bullfrog was
   - □ a. ladylike.
   - □ b. a poor businessman.
   - □ c. rough and unsophisticated.

5. Thomas Bullfrog wanted to marry a lady who had
   - □ a. pearly teeth.
   - □ b. a virgin heart.
   - □ c. both a and b.

Understanding the Passage

6. In regards to marriage, the narrator felt that many men
   - □ a. were too fussy.
   - □ b. lacked discrimination.
   - □ c. married too soon.

7. The narrator felt that
   - □ a. most women were close to perfect.
   - □ b. men should not wait too long to marry.
   - □ c. marriage should be avoided at all costs.

8. The narrator thought that all minor objections should be
   - □ a. directly confronted.
   - □ b. resolved before marriage.
   - □ c. ignored.

9. The narrator
   - □ a. was speaking from personal experience.
   - □ b. married at an early age.
   - □ c. both a and b.

10. As a young man, Thomas Bullfrog appeared to be
    - □ a. very vain.
    - □ b. naive about human nature.
    - □ c. indelicate.

If I say, that in any creature breathing is only a function indispensable to vitality, inasmuch as it withdraws from the air a certain element, which being subsequently brought into contact with the blood imparts to the blood its vivifying principle, I do not think I shall err; though I may possibly use some superfluous scientific words. Assume it, and it follows that if all the blood in a man could be aerated with one breath, he might then seal up his nostrils and not fetch another for a considerable time—in other words, he would then live without breathing. Anomalous as it may seem, this is precisely the case with the whale, who systematically lives, by intervals, his complete hour and more (when at the bottom) without drawing a single breath, or in any way inhaling a particle of air; for remember, he has no gills. Instead, between his ribs and on each side of his spine, he is supplied with a remarkable involved labyrinth of vermicelli-like vessels; these vessels, when he quits the surface, are completely distended with oxygenated blood. So that for an hour or longer, a thousand fathoms in the sea, he carries a surplus stock of vitality in him, just as the camel crossing the waterless desert carries a surplus supply of drink for future use in its four supplementary stomachs. The anatomical fact of this labyrinth is indisputable; and that the supposition founded upon it is reasonable and true, appears the more cogent to me, when I consider the otherwise inexplicable obstinacy of that leviathan in *having his spoutings out*, as the fishermen phrase it. This is what I mean: if unmolested, upon rising to the surface, the sperm whale will continue there for a period of time exactly uniform with all his other unmolested risings. Say he stays eleven minutes, and jets seventy times, that is, respires seventy breaths; then whenever he rises again, he will be absolutely sure to have his seventy breaths over again, to a minute. Now, if after he fetches a few breaths you alarm him, so that he sounds, he will be always dodging up again to make good his regular allowance of air, and not until those seventy breaths are told, will he finally go down to spend his full term below. Remark, however, that in different individuals these rates are different; but in any one they are alike.

Recalling Facts

1. A whale gets the elements it needs for vitality when air comes in contact with its
   - □ a. heart.
   - □ b. liver.
   - □ c. blood.

2. A whale can stay under water for
   - □ a. a few minutes.
   - □ b. half an hour.
   - □ c. an hour or longer.

3. A camel carries its extra water in supplementary
   - □ a. stomachs.
   - □ b. intestines.
   - □ c. kidneys.

4. If undisturbed, the sperm whale will stay on the surface
   - □ a. only a few moments.
   - □ b. a precise period of time.
   - □ c. an hour or longer.

5. "Having its spoutings out" refers to the whale's
   - □ a. breathing pattern.
   - □ b. rapid diving.
   - □ c. lung capacity.

Understanding the Passage

6. The narrator appears to speak as someone
   - □ a. unfamiliar with whales.
   - □ b. new to the world of whales.
   - □ c. knowledgeable about whales.

7. One thing whales can do much better than humans is
   - □ a. defend themselves.
   - □ b. feed their young.
   - □ c. hold their breath.

8. The narrator was trying to explain the whale's need to
   - □ a. live deep beneath the surface.
   - □ b. swim near fishing boats
   - □ c. spout a fixed number of times.

9. A whale's habits are
   - □ a. puzzling.
   - □ b. unaffected by whale hunters.
   - □ c. extremely regular.

10. The whale would be much more difficult to hunt if it had
    - □ a. a smaller spout.
    - □ b. more blood.
    - □ c. gills.

The first settlers of this colony were Englishmen, loyal subjects to their king and church, and the grant to Sir Walter Raleigh contained an express Proviso that their laws "should not be against the true Christian faith, now professed in the church of England." As soon as the state of the colony admitted, it was divided into parishes, in each of which was established a minister of the Anglican church, endowed with a fixed salary, in tobacco, a glebe house and land with the other necessary appendages. To meet these expenses all the inhabitants of the parishes were assessed, whether they were or not members of the established church. Towards Quakers who came here they were most cruelly intolerant, driving them from the colony by the severest penalties. In process of time, however, other sectarisms were introduced, chiefly of the Presbyterian family; and the established clergy, secure for life in their globes and salaries, adding to these generally the emoluments of a classical school, found employment enough, in their farms and schoolrooms for the rest of the week, and devoted Sunday only to the edification of their flock, by service, and a sermon at their parish church. Their other pastoral functions were little attended to. Against this inactivity the zeal and industry of sectarian preachers had an open and undisputed field; and by the time of the revolution, a majority of the inhabitants had become dissenters from the established church, but were still obliged to pay contributions to support the pastors of the minority. This unrighteous compulsion to maintain teachers of what they deemed religious errors was grievously felt during the regal government. The first republican legislature which met in 1776 was crowded with petitions to abolish this spiritual tyranny. These brought on the severest contests in which I have ever been engaged. Our great opponents were Mr. Pendleton & Robert Carter Nicholas, honest men, but zealous churchmen. The petitions were referred to the committee of the whole house on the state of the country; and after desperate contests in that committee, almost daily from the 11th of October to the 5th of December, we prevailed so far only as to repeal the laws which rendered criminal the maintenance of any religious opinions, the forbearance of repairing to church, or the exercise of any mode of worship: and further, to exempt dissenters from contributions to the support of the established church.

Recalling Facts

1. The first settlers of the colony were
   - ☐ a. Quakers.
   - ☐ b. Englishmen.
   - ☐ c. Dutchmen.

2. Ministers of the Anglican church received a fixed salary in
   - ☐ a. gold.
   - ☐ b. corn.
   - ☐ c. tobacco.

3. Early Quakers were treated
   - ☐ a. as oddities.
   - ☐ b. kindly.
   - ☐ c. cruelly.

4. Most of the dissenting sects were of the
   - ☐ a. Presbyterian family.
   - ☐ b. Methodist family.
   - ☐ c. Baptist family.

5. Mr. Pendleton was described as
   - ☐ a. a zealous churchman.
   - ☐ b. a devoted father.
   - ☐ c. an inactive preacher.

Understanding the Passage

6. In the early days of the colony, Anglican ministers had
   - ☐ a. financial security.
   - ☐ b. a demanding schedule.
   - ☐ c. many political responsibilities.

7. The narrator characterized Anglican ministers as
   - ☐ a. neglectful of their religious duties.
   - ☐ b. brave soldiers of the revolution.
   - ☐ c. highly critical of the king.

8. Robert Carter Nicholas defended the law requiring
   - ☐ a. ministers to earn income outside the church.
   - ☐ b. Quakers to swear allegiance to the king of England.
   - ☐ c. everyone to support the Anglican church.

9. Dissenting preachers apparently
   - ☐ a. found little support in the colony.
   - ☐ b. worked hard to serve their flock.
   - ☐ c. condemned the revolution.

10. The committee on the state of the country witnessed
    - ☐ a. much heated debate.
    - ☐ b. several embarrassing confessions.
    - ☐ c. the resignation of several office holders.

It is a subject of curious inquiry at the present day to look into the brief records of America's early colonial period and observe how regular, and with few exceptions how inevitable, were the gradations, on the one hand, of the masters to poverty, and on the other, of their servants to wealth. Accustomed to ease and unequal to the struggles incident to an infant society, the affluent emigrant was barely enabled to maintain his own rank by the weight of his personal superiority and acquirements; but the moment that his head was laid in the grave, his indolent and comparatively unedu- ●
cated offspring were compelled to yield precedency to the more active energies of a class whose exertions had been stimulated by necessity. This is a very common course of things, even in the present state of the Union; but it was peculiarly the fortunes of the two extremes of society in the peaceful and unenterprising colonies of Pennsylvania and New Jersey.

The posterity of Marmaduke did not escape the common lot of those who depend rather on their hereditary possessions than on their powers, and in the third generation they had descended to a point below which, in this happy country, it is barely possible for honesty, intellect, and ●
sobriety to fall. The same pride of family that had, by its self-satisfied indolence, conduced to aid their fall now became a principle to stimulate them to endeavor to rise again. The feeling, from being morbid, was changed to a healthful and active desire to emulate the character, the condition, and, with luck, the wealth of their ancestors also. It was the father of our new acquaintance, the Judge, who first began to reascend in the scale of society; and in this undertaking he was not a little assisted by ●
a marriage which aided in furnishing the means of educating his only son in a rather better manner than the low state of the common schools in Pennsylvania could promise, or than had been the practice of the family for the two or three preceding generations.

At the school where the reviving prosperity of his father was enabled to maintain him, the young Marmaduke formed an intimacy with a youth whose years were about equal to his own. This was a fortunate connection for our Judge and paved the way to most of his future elevation in life.

Recalling Facts

1. The narrator regarded
   Pennsylvania and
   New Jersey as
   □ a. troublesome.
   □ b. unenterprising.
   □ c. democratic.

2. The original Marmaduke was
   born into the
   □ a. upper class.
   □ b. middle class.
   □ c. lower class.

3. The descendants of
   Marmaduke hit rock
   bottom after
   □ a. two generations.
   □ b. three generations.
   □ c. four generations.

4. The father of the Judge
   □ a. was the first to reascend
       the scale of society.
   □ b. caused the downfall of
       his family.
   □ c. married a penniless
       immigrant.

5. At school, the Judge had the
   good fortune to
   □ a. join the top fraternal
       order.
   □ b. meet an important friend.
   □ c. succeed in all his studies.

Understanding the Passage

6. In early America, the family of
   a rich emigrant tended to
   □ a. do poorly.
   □ b. become richer.
   □ c. gain control of the local
       government.

7. In an infant society, talent
   and fortitude were
   □ a. useless.
   □ b. important.
   □ c. often forgotten.

8. The first few generations of
   Marmaduke's descendants
   □ a. did not strive to
       improve their positions.
   □ b. all became exceedingly rich
   □ c. lost only a little of the
       family's power.

9. After a while, the family
   □ a. simply died out.
   □ b. had no place to
       go but up.
   □ c. returned to Europe.

10. The young Marmaduke
    □ a. attended a public school.
    □ b. went to a private school.
    □ c. was tutored at home.

Teresa, Mrs. Thropplestance, was the richest and most intractable old woman in the county of Woldshire. In her dealings with the world in general her manner suggested a blend between a Mistress of the Robes and a Master of Foxhounds, with the vocabulary of both. In her domestic circle she comported herself in the arbitrary style that one attributes, probably without the least justification, to an American political Boss in the bosom of his caucus. The late Theodore Thropplestance had left her, some thirty-five years ago, in absolute possession of a considerable fortune, a large landed property, and a gallery full of valuable pictures. In those intervening years she had outlived her son and quarreled with her elder grandson, who had married without her consent or approval. Bertie Thropplestance, her younger grandson, was the heir-designate to her property, and as such he was a center of interest and concern to some half-hundred ambitious mothers with daughters of marriageable age. Bertie was an amiable, easygoing young man, who was quite ready to marry anyone who was favorably recommended to his notice, but he was not going to waste his time in falling in love with anyone who would come under his grandmother's veto. The favorable recommendation would have to come from Mrs. Thropplestance.

Teresa's house parties were always rounded off with a plentiful garnishing of presentable young women and alert, attendant mothers, but the old lady was emphatically discouraging whenever any one of her girl guests became at all likely to outbid the others as a possible granddaughter-in-law. It was the inheritance of her fortune and estate that was in question, and she was evidently disposed to exercise and enjoy her powers of selection and rejection to the utmost. Bertie's preferences did not greatly matter; he was of the sort who can be stolidly happy with any kind of wife; he had cheerfully put up with his grandmother all his life, so he was not likely to fret and fume over anything that might befall him in the way of a helpmate.

The party that gathered under Teresa's roof in Christmas week of the year nineteen hundred and something was of smaller proportions than usual, and Mrs. Yonelet, who formed one of the party, was inclined to deduce hopeful augury from this circumstance. Dora Yonalet and Bertie were so obviously made for one another, she confided to the vicar's wife.

Recalling Facts

1. Teresa was known for being
   - ☐ a. flexible.
   - ☐ b. generous.
   - ☐ c. arbitrary.

2. Theodore Thropplestance had been dead for
   - ☐ a. five years.
   - ☐ b. fifteen years.
   - ☐ c. thirty-five years.

3. Teresa's son was now
   - ☐ a. engaged to be married.
   - ☐ b. married without her blessing.
   - ☐ c. dead.

4. Teresa planned to will her property to her
   - ☐ a. late son's estate.
   - ☐ b. elder grandson.
   - ☐ c. younger grandson.

5. The most recent Christmas party was
   - ☐ a. smaller than usual.
   - ☐ b. similar in size to past parties.
   - ☐ c. larger than usual.

Understanding the Passage

6. Teresa appeared to be
   - ☐ a. a kindly old lady.
   - ☐ b. an assertive and confident woman.
   - ☐ c. on the edge of senility.

7. Teresa was disappointed by her older grandson's choice of a
   - ☐ a. wife.
   - ☐ b. country manor.
   - ☐ c. profession.

8. Bertie could easily
   - ☐ a. defy his grandmother.
   - ☐ b. find someone who wanted to marry him.
   - ☐ c. get married to anyone he chose.

9. Teresa wanted to
   - ☐ a. hasten Bertie's marriage
   - ☐ b. continue to exercise her power over her estate.
   - ☐ c. please one of the anxious mothers.

10. In terms of selecting a wife, Bertie was
    - ☐ a. painfully shy.
    - ☐ b. determined to follow his heart.
    - ☐ c. extremely flexible.

To one of middle age the countenance of Yeobright was that of a young man, though a youth might hardly have seen any necessity for the term of immaturity; but it was really one of those faces which convey less the idea of so many years as its age than of so much experience as its store. The number of their years may have adequately summed up Jared, Mahalaleel, and the rest of the antediluvians, but the age of a modern man is to be measured by the intensity of his history.

The face was well shaped, even excellently, but the mind within was ● beginning to use it as a mere waste tablet whereon to trace its idiosyncrasies as they developed themselves. The beauty here visible would in no long time be ruthlessly overrun by its parasite, thought, which might just as well have fed upon a plainer exterior where there was nothing it could harm. Had Heaven preserved Yeobright from a wearing habit of meditation, people would have said, "A handsome man;" had his brain unfolded under sharper contours they would have said, "A thoughtful man;" but an inner strenuousness was preying upon an outer symmetry, and they classified ● his look as singular.

Hence people who began by beholding him ended by perusing him. His countenance was overlaid with legible meanings. Without being thought-worn he yet had certain marks derived from a perception of his surroundings, such as are not infrequently found on individuals at the end of the four or five years of endeavor which follow the close of placid pupilage. He already showed that thought is a disease of flesh, and indirectly bore evidence that ideal physical beauty is incompatible with emotional development and a full recognition of the coil of things. Mental luminousness must be fed with the oil of life, even though there is already a physical ● need for it; and the pitiful sight of two demands on one supply was just showing itself here.

When standing before certain men the philosopher regrets that thinkers are but perishable tissue, the artist that perishable tissue has to think. Thus to deplore, each from his own particular point of view, the mutually destructive interdependence of spirit and flesh would have been instinctive with these in critically observing Yeobright.

As for his look, it was a natural cheerfulness striving against depression from without, and not quite succeeding.

Recalling Facts

1. The narrator feels that the age of a modern man must be measured by the
   - ☐ a. number of his years.
   - ☐ b. intensity of his history.
   - ☐ c. cheerfulness of his expression.

2. The narrator contends that the parasite of beauty is
   - ☐ a. envy.
   - ☐ b. greed.
   - ☐ c. thought.

3. Yeobright's face was
   - ☐ a. well shaped.
   - ☐ b. marred by lack of sleep.
   - ☐ c. dull and impassive.

4. According to the narrator, philosophers often regret that
   - ☐ a. thinkers are but perishable tissue.
   - ☐ b. perishable tissue has to think.
   - ☐ c. spirit and flesh are not more interdependent.

5. The narrator believes that thought is
   - ☐ a. vital to inner and outer beauty.
   - ☐ b. the oil of life.
   - ☐ c. a disease of flesh.

Understanding the Passage

6. According to the narrator, Yeobright's physical beauty would
   - ☐ a. soon be his only source of happiness.
   - ☐ b. not last much longer.
   - ☐ c. cause his downfall.

7. The narrator felt that Yeobright's beauty was
   - ☐ a. being destroyed by the strain of thinking.
   - ☐ b. responsible for his mental luminousness.
   - ☐ c. common in men who engaged in physical labor.

8. Yeobright apparently valued
   - ☐ a. honesty more than wealth.
   - ☐ b. thought more than beauty.
   - ☐ c. beauty more than companionship.

9. The narrator believes that thought and beauty
   - ☐ a. cannot coexist in the same person for very long.
   - ☐ b. are both necessary to comprehend the coil of life
   - ☐ c. each work to destroy an individual's instincts.

10. Yeobright was already showing signs of
   - ☐ a. the strain of mental activity.
   - ☐ b. becoming a great artist.
   - ☐ c. rejecting the wisdom of philosophers.

There are few persons, even among the calmest thinkers, who have not occasionally been startled into a vague yet thrilling half-credence in the supernatural, by *coincidences* of so seemingly marvelous a character that, as *mere* coincidences, the intellect has been unable to receive them. Such sentiments—for the half-credences of which I speak have never the full force of *thought*—such sentiments are seldom thoroughly stifled unless by reference to the doctrine of chance, or, as it is technically termed, the Calculus of Probabilities. Now this Calculus is, in its essence, purely mathematical; and thus we have the anomaly of the most rigidly exact in science applied to the shadow and spirituality of the most intangible in speculation.

The extraordinary details which I am now called upon to make public, will be found to form, as regards sequence of time, the primary branch of a series of scarcely intelligible *coincidences*, whose secondary or concluding branch will be recognized by all readers in the late murder of MARY CECILIA ROGERS, at New York.

When, in an article entitled *The Murders in the Rue Morgue*, I endeavored, about a year ago, to depict some very remarkable features in the mental character of my friend, the Chevalier C. Auguste Dupin, it did not occur to me that I should ever resume the subject. This depicting of character constituted my design; and this design was thoroughly fulfilled in the wild train of circumstances brought to instance Dupin's idiosyncrasy. I might have adduced other examples, but I should have proven no more. Late events, however, in their surprising development, have startled me into some further details, which will carry with them the air of extorted confession. Hearing what I have lately heard, it would be indeed strange should I remain silent in regard to what I both heard and saw so long ago.

Upon the winding up of the tragedy involved in the deaths of Madame L'Espanaye and her daughter, the Chevalier dismissed the affair at once from his attention, and relapsed into his old habits of moody revery. Prone, at all times, to abstraction, I readily fell in with his humor; and continuing to occupy our chambers in the Faubourg Saint Germain, we gave the Future to the winds, and slumbered tranquilly in the Present, weaving the dull world around us into dreams.

But these dreams were not altogether uninterrupted.

Recalling Facts

1. The Calculus of Probabilities
   is another term for
   ☐ a. thought.
   ☐ b. chance.
   ☐ c. the supernatural.

2. The Calculus of
   Probabilities is
   ☐ a. inflexible.
   ☐ b. purely mathematical.
   ☐ c. completely intangible.

3. Mary Cecilia Rogers was
   ☐ a. wealthy.
   ☐ b. vacationing.
   ☐ c. murdered.

4. The Chevalier C. Auguste
   Dupin was the narrator's
   ☐ a. friend.
   ☐ b. brother.
   ☐ c. father.

5. The Chevalier was always
   prone to
   ☐ a. mental seizures.
   ☐ b. moody revery.
   ☐ c. angry outbursts.

Understanding the Passage

6. Half-credence refers to the
   idea that most people
   ☐ a. cannot completely
        dismiss the concept of
        the supernatural.
   ☐ b. use a formal way of
        thinking and reasoning.
   ☐ c. believe in the Calculus
        of Probabilities.

7. The narrator sees an
   inconsistency when applying
   the laws of chance to
   ☐ a. solving a murder.
   ☐ b. dreaming about tragedies.
   ☐ c. the world of the
        supernatural.

8. After writing about the
   character of Dupin, the
   narrator intended to
   ☐ a. solve the murder.
   ☐ b. drop the subject.
   ☐ c. study the laws of
        probability.

9. The narrator has apparently
   ☐ a. heard something new.
   ☐ b. confessed to a crime.
   ☐ c. dismissed Dupin.

10. The narrator
    ☐ a. had no further use for Dupin
    ☐ b. easily adapated to Dupin's
         moods.
    ☐ c. dismissed the death of
         Madame L'Espanaye.

47 *from* **The Life of Samuel Johnson** *by James Boswell*

1763 is to me a memorable year; for in it I had the happiness to obtain the acquaintance of that extraordinary man whose memoirs I am now writing, an acquaintance which I shall ever esteem as one of the most fortunate circumstances in my life. Though then but two-and-twenty, I had for several years read his works with delight and instruction and had the highest reverence for their author, which had grown up in my fancy into a kind of mysterious veneration, by figuring to myself a state of solemn elevated abstraction in which I supposed him to live in the immense metropolis of London. Mr. Gentleman, a native of Ireland, who passed some years in Scotland as a player and as an instructor in the English language, had given me a representation of the figure and manner of Dictionary Johnson! as he was then generally called; and during my first visit to London, which was for three months in 1760, Mr. Derrick the poet, who was Gentleman's friend and countryman, flattered me with hopes that he would introduce me to Johnson, an honor of which I was very ambitious. But he never found an opportunity, which made me doubt that he had promised to do what was not in his power; till Johnson some years afterwards told me, "Derrick, Sir, might very well have introduced you. I had a kindness for Derrick and am sorry he is dead."

In the summer of 1761 Mr. Thomas Sheridan was at Edinburgh and delivered lectures upon the English language and Public Speaking to respectable audiences. I was often in his company and heard him frequently expatiate upon Johnson's extraordinary knowledge, talents, and virtues; repeat his pointed sayings, describe his particularities, and boast of his being his guest sometimes till three in the morning. At his house I hoped to have many opportunities of seeing the sage, as Mr. Sheridan obligingly assured me I should not be disappointed.

When I returned to London in the end of 1762, to my surprise and regret I found an irreconcilable difference had taken place between Johnson and Sheridan. A pension of two hundred pounds a year had been given to Sheridan. Johnson who, as has been already mentioned, thought slightingly of Sheridan's art, upon hearing that he was also pensioned, exclaimed, "What! Have they given *him* a pension? Then it is time for me to give up mine."

Recalling Facts

1. The narrator was writing
   - ☐ a. an autobiography.
   - ☐ b. a historical novel.
   - ☐ c. memoirs of another person.

2. Mr. Gentleman once
   - ☐ a. taught English.
   - ☐ b. played professional soccer.
   - ☐ c. wrote a dictionary.

3. Mr. Derrick promised to introduce the narrator to
   - ☐ a. Gentleman.
   - ☐ b. Sheridan.
   - ☐ c. Johnson.

4. At the time this passage was written, Derrick was
   - ☐ a. living in Edinburgh.
   - ☐ b. dead.
   - ☐ c. in seclusion.

5. Johnson was upset that Sheridan had been given
   - ☐ a. a pension.
   - ☐ b. a royal appointment.
   - ☐ c. credit for work he hadn't written.

Understanding the Passage

6. The narrator enjoyed 1763 because that was the year he
   - ☐ a. got to know Johnson.
   - ☐ b. taught with Gentleman in Scotland.
   - ☐ c. collaborated on a history book with Sheridan.

7. Johnson informed the narrator of Derrick's
   - ☐ a. underhanded ways.
   - ☐ b. talent.
   - ☐ c. honesty.

8. The narrator appeared to be
   - ☐ a. a close friend of Johnson.
   - ☐ b. in awe of Johnson.
   - ☐ c. distrustful of Johnson.

9. Johnson thought that Sheridan was
   - ☐ a. quite talented.
   - ☐ b. overrated.
   - ☐ c. unlucky in financial matters.

10. Until 1762, Sheridan
    - ☐ a. did not know Johnson personally.
    - ☐ b. had met Johnson but once.
    - ☐ c. thought highly of Johnson.

The schoolmaster is generally a man of some importance in the female circle of a rural neighborhood, being considered a kind of idle gentleman-like personage, of vastly superior taste and accomplishments to the rough country swains, and, indeed, inferior in learning only to the parson. His appearance, therefore, is apt to occasion some little stir at the tea table of a farmhouse, and the addition of a supernumerary dish of cakes or sweet-meats, or, peradventure, the parade of a silver teapot. Our man of letters, therefore, was peculiarly happy in the smiles of all the country damsels. He figured prominently among them in the churchyard, between services on Sundays; gathering grapes for them from the wild vines that overrun the surrounding trees; reciting for their amusement all the epitaphs on the tombstones, or sauntering, with a whole bevy of them, along the banks of the adjacent mill pond; while the more bashful country bumpkins hung sheepishly back, envying his superior elegance and address.

From his half-itinerant life, also, he was a kind of traveling gazette, carrying the whole budget of local gossip from farmhouse to farmhouse; so that his appearance was always greeted with satisfaction. He was, moreover, esteemed by the women as a man of great erudition, for he had read several books quite thoroughly, and was a perfect master of Cotton Mather's History of New England Witchcraft, in which, by the way, he most firmly and potently believed.

He was, in fact, an odd mixture of small shrewdness and simple credulity. His appetite for the marvelous, and his powers of digesting it, were equally extraordinary; and both had been increased by his residence in this spell-bound region. No tale was too gross or monstrous for his capacious swallow, and it was often his delight, after his school was dismissed of an afternoon, to stretch himself on the rich bed of clover, bordering the little brook that whimpered by his schoolhouse, and there con over old Mather's direful tales, until the gathering dusk of evening made the printed page a mere mist before his eyes. Then, as he wended his way, by swamp and stream and awful woodland, to the farmhouse where he happened to be quartered, every sound of nature, at that witching hour, fluttered his excited imagination: the moaning of the whippoorwill; the boding cry of the tree toad; or the dreary hooting of the screech owl.

Recalling Facts

1. The schoolmaster was considered to be a superior person by the
   - ☐ a. schoolchildren.
   - ☐ b. females in the village.
   - ☐ c. other men his age.

2. The schoolmaster was a particular center of interest
   - ☐ a. between church services.
   - ☐ b. at literary gatherings.
   - ☐ c. on hunting and fishing trips.

3. For the ladies' amusement, the schoolmaster read
   - ☐ a. the Bible in Latin.
   - ☐ b. tombstones.
   - ☐ c. the diaries of young females.

4. The schoolmaster believed in
   - ☐ a. witchcraft.
   - ☐ b. strict discipline.
   - ☐ c. daily walks.

5. The schoolmaster loved to reflect on
   - ☐ a. his own brilliant mind.
   - ☐ b. Mather's tales.
   - ☐ c. the trickling brook.

Understanding the Passage

6. Most men in the area did not have the schoolmaster's
   - ☐ a. riches.
   - ☐ b. political connections.
   - ☐ c. self-assurance.

7. When visiting local farm-houses, the schoolmaster was
   - ☐ a. treated as an important guest.
   - ☐ b. expected to do his share of the chores.
   - ☐ c. often met with hostility and distrust.

8. The schoolmaster knew all the
   - ☐ a. news around town.
   - ☐ b. compositions of Mozart.
   - ☐ c. famous educators of his time.

9. The schoolmaster spent much of his free time
   - ☐ a. courting wealthy widows
   - ☐ b. reading in the woods.
   - ☐ c. doing healthy exercises.

10. Apparently, the schoolmaster enjoyed
    - ☐ a. hunting and fishing.
    - ☐ b. the attention of women.
    - ☐ c. downplaying his accomplishments.

During the entire night, sleeping or waking, images of the fair Berenice Montenero were continually recurring in an unbelievably provoking manner. At breakfast my mother did not appear; my father announced that she hadn't slept well, and that she would breakfast in her own apartment; this wasn't unusual; but I was particularly sorry that it happened this morning, because being left alone with my father, and he full of a debate on the malt tax, which he undertook to read to me from the rival newspapers, and to make me understand its merits, I was compelled to sit three-quarters of an hour longer after breakfast than I had intended; so that the plan I had formed of waiting upon Berenice's father, Mr. Montenero, very early, before he could have gone out for the day, was disconcerted. When at last my father had fairly finished, when he had taken his cane, and departing left me as I thought happily at liberty, another detainer came. At the foot of the stairs my mother's woman appeared, waiting to tell me that her lady begged I would not go out till she had seen me—adding, that she would be presentable in less than a quarter of an hour.

I flung down my hat, I believe, with rather too marked an expression of impatience; but five minutes afterwards came a knock at the door. Mr. Montenero was announced, and I blessed my mother, my father, and the malt tax, for having detained me at home. The first appearance of Mr. Montenero more than answered my expectations: he had that indescribable air which, independently of the fashion of the day, or the mode of any particular country, distinguishes a gentleman—dignified, courteous, and totally free from affectation. From his figure, he might have been thought a Spaniard—from his complexion, an East Indian; but he had a peculiar cast of countenance, which seemed not to belong to either nation. He had uncommonly black penetrating eyes, with a serious, rather melancholy, but very benevolent expression. He was past the meridian of life. The lines in his face were strongly marked; but they were not the commonplace wrinkles of ignoble age, nor the contractions of any vulgar passions: they seemed to be the traces of thought and feeling. He entered into conversation directly and easily. I needn't say his conversation was immediately interesting, for he spoke of Berenice.

Recalling Facts

1. During the night, the narrator continuously thought of
   - ☐ a. his ailing mother.
   - ☐ b. Berenice Montenero.
   - ☐ c. his plan for meeting Mr. Montenero.

2. At breakfast the father announced that the mother
   - ☐ a. had not slept well.
   - ☐ b. was upstairs with the doctor.
   - ☐ c. forbid him to leave without seeing her.

3. The father engaged the narrator in a discussion of the
   - ☐ a. quality of rival newspapers.
   - ☐ b. current fashions in Spain.
   - ☐ c. malt tax.

4. The narrator ended up meeting Mr. Montenero
   - ☐ a. in Mr. Montenero's home.
   - ☐ b. at his father's office.
   - ☐ c. in the narrator's home.

5. Mr. Montenero's face was
   - ☐ a. bright and open.
   - ☐ b. marked with strong lines.
   - ☐ c. dark and menacing.

Understanding the Passage

6. The narrrator's father was unaware of the narrator's
   - ☐ a. support for the malt tax.
   - ☐ b. political inclinations.
   - ☐ c. desire to hurry through breakfast.

7. The narrator was most eager to talk to
   - ☐ a. his father.
   - ☐ b. his mother.
   - ☐ c. Mr. Montenero.

8. Upon receiving the message to wait for his mother, the narrator became
   - ☐ a. confused.
   - ☐ b. annoyed.
   - ☐ c. nervous.

9. The narrator felt Mr. Montenero was
   - ☐ a. a thoughtful and honorable man.
   - ☐ b. deceitful and underhanded.
   - ☐ c. incapable of under-standing complexities.

10. Mr. Montenero was not
    - ☐ a. a young man.
    - ☐ b. really Berenice's father.
    - ☐ c. able to speak to the narrator.

During the next three weeks Newman saw Bellegarde several times, and without formally swearing an eternal friendship the two men established a sort of comradeship. To Newman, Bellegarde was the ideal Frenchman, the Frenchman of tradition and romance, so far as our hero was acquainted with these mystical influences. Gallant, expansive, amusing, more pleased himself with the effort he produced than those (even when they were well pleased) for whom he produced it; a master of all the distinctively social virtues and a votary of all agreeable sensations; a devotee of something mysterious and sacred to which he occasionally alluded in terms more ecstatic even than those in which he spoke of the last pretty woman, and which was simply the beautiful though somewhat superannuated image of *honor;* he was irresistably entertaining and enlivening, and he formed a character to which Newman was as capable of doing justice when he had once been placed in contact with it, as he was unlikely, in musing upon the possible mixtures of our human ingredients, mentally to have fore-shadowed it. Bellegarde did not in the least cause him to modify his needful premise that all Frenchmen are of a frothy and imponderable substance; he simply reminded him that light materials may be beaten up into a most agreeable compound. No two companions could be more different, but their differences made a capital basis for a friendship of which the distinctive characteristic was that it was extremely amusing to each.

Valentin de Bellegarde lived in the basement of an old house in the Rue d'Anjou St. Honoré, and his small apartments lay between the court of the house and an old garden which spread itself behind it—one of those large, sunless, humid gardens into which you look unexpectingly in Paris from back windows, wondering how among the grudging habitations they find their space. When Newman returned Bellegarde's visit, he hinted that *his* lodging was at least as much a laughing matter as his own. But its oddities were of a different cast from those of our hero's gilded saloons on the Boulevard Haussmann: the place was low, dusky, contracted, and crowded with curious bric-a-brac. Bellegarde, penniless patrician as he was, was an insatiable collector, and his walls were covered with rusty arms and ancient panels and platters, his doorways draped in faded tapestries, his floors muffled in the skins of beasts.

Recalling Facts

1. Newman viewed Bellegarde as
   - ☐ a. an ideal Frenchman.
   - ☐ b. a French outlaw.
   - ☐ c. a member of the French aristocracy.

2. Newman considered all Frenchmen to be
   - ☐ a. disrespectful.
   - ☐ b. cowardly.
   - ☐ c. imponderable.

3. Newman and Bellegarde became
   - ☐ a. partners.
   - ☐ b. friends.
   - ☐ c. rivals.

4. Bellegarde lived in
   - ☐ a. a townhouse.
   - ☐ b. the basement of an old house.
   - ☐ c. a guest cottage.

5. Newman lived
   - ☐ a. on the Boulevard Haussmann.
   - ☐ b. in the Rue d'Anjou St. Honoré.
   - ☐ c. on the island of Corsica.

Understanding the Passage

6. Newman wanted to find in Bellegarde a
   - ☐ a. likely assassin.
   - ☐ b. romantic personality.
   - ☐ c. rich patron.

7. Bellegarde appears to be
   - ☐ a. well educated.
   - ☐ b. rich, but boring.
   - ☐ c. sober and puritanical.

8. Newman
   - ☐ a. was not French.
   - ☐ b. came from a similar background as Bellegarde.
   - ☐ c. could not speak French fluently.

9. Newman and Bellegarde shared
   - ☐ a. the same house.
   - ☐ b. pleasant conversation.
   - ☐ c. the same circle of old friends.

10. Newman's apartment was probably
   - ☐ a. quite unlike Bellegarde's.
   - ☐ b. tastefully decorated.
   - ☐ c. part of a former rich estate

Answer Key

Progress Graph

Pacing Graph

Answer Key

1	1. b	2. a	3. c	4. a	5. c	6. a	7. c	8. b	9. b	10. b
2	1. a	2. b	3. c	4. b	5. c	6. a	7. b	8. c	9. b	10. a
3	1. b	2. c	3. a	4. c	5. c	6. a	7. b	8. a	9. a	10. a
4	1. c	2. a	3. b	4. a	5. b	6. c	7. a	8. a	9. b	10. c
5	1. c	2. b	3. c	4. a	5. a	6. a	7. a	8. b	9. b	10. a
6	1. a	2. c	3. b	4. c	5. b	6. a	7. a	8. c	9. b	10. a
7	1. b	2. a	3. b	4. a	5. b	6. b	7. b	8. a	9. c	10. a
8	1. a	2. c	3. b	4. a	5. c	6. b	7. a	8. a	9. c	10. c
9	1. c	2. c	3. c	4. a	5. b	6. b	7. c	8. a	9. a	10. c
10	1. a	2. c	3. b	4. c	5. c	6. a	7. b	8. c	9. b	10. a
11	1. c	2. c	3. b	4. b	5. c	6. b	7. c	8. c	9. c	10. b
12	1. c	2. a	3. c	4. a	5. c	6. b	7. a	8. a	9. c	10. c
13	1. b	2. c	3. c	4. a	5. c	6. b	7. a	8. a	9. c	10. a
14	1. c	2. a	3. b	4. a	5. c	6. a	7. a	8. a	9. b	10. c
15	1. b	2. b	3. c	4. c	5. a	6. a	7. b	8. c	9. a	10. c
16	1. a	2. b	3. a	4. b	5. a	6. b	7. a	8. c	9. b	10. a
17	1. c	2. a	3. a	4. c	5. c	6. b	7. b	8. b	9. a	10. b
18	1. a	2. a	3. b	4. b	5. a	6. a	7. b	8. c	9. c	10. b
19	1. c	2. a	3. a	4. b	5. a	6. a	7. b	8. b	9. c	10. c
20	1. c	2. a	3. c	4. a	5. b	6. b	7. a	8. a	9. a	10. c
21	1. c	2. b	3. a	4. b	5. c	6. a	7. b	8. a	9. c	10. a
22	1. b	2. c	3. a	4. c	5. c	6. b	7. c	8. a	9. a	10. c
23	1. a	2. a	3. c	4. c	5. a	6. b	7. c	8. b	9. b	10. b
24	1. a	2. b	3. c	4. c	5. c	6. b	7. a	8. b	9. b	10. a
25	1. c	2. b	3. b	4. b	5. b	6. a	7. c	8. c	9. a	10. c

26	1. a	2. c	3. c	4. a	5. a	6. b	7. a	8. b	9. b	10. b
27	1. a	2. c	3. a	4. b	5. c	6. a	7. b	8. a	9. a	10. b
28	1. b	2. c	3. c	4. a	5. b	6. c	7. c	8. a	9. b	10. a
29	1. a	2. c	3. a	4. b	5. c	6. a	7. b	8. c	9. a	10. a
30	1. a	2. b	3. c	4. a	5. c	6. c	7. c	8. b	9. b	10. b
31	1. c	2. b	3. a	4. a	5. b	6. b	7. b	8. c	9. c	10. a
32	1. b	2. a	3. b	4. c	5. c	6. c	7. a	8. a	9. c	10. a
33	1. b	2. a	3. c	4. c	5. a	6. b	7. a	8. a	9. b	10. b
34	1. a	2. c	3. b	4. b	5. b	6. c	7. a	8. c	9. a	10. b
35	1. c	2. b	3. a	4. b	5. b	6. b	7. c	8. c	9. a	10. c
36	1. c	2. a	3. a	4. a	5. b	6. b	7. a	8. c	9. c	10. c
37	1. b	2. c	3. b	4. b	5. a	6. a	7. a	8. a	9. a	10. b
38	1. a	2. c	3. a	4. b	5. c	6. a	7. a	8. c	9. b	10. b
39	1. a	2. c	3. b	4. b	5. a	6. a	7. b	8. b	9. c	10. c
40	1. c	2. b	3. b	4. a	5. c	6. a	7. b	8. c	9. a	10. a
41	1. c	2. c	3. a	4. b	5. a	6. c	7. c	8. c	9. c	10. c
42	1. b	2. c	3. c	4. a	5. a	6. a	7. a	8. c	9. b	10. a
43	1. b	2. a	3. b	4. a	5. b	6. a	7. b	8. a	9. b	10. b
44	1. c	2. c	3. c	4. c	5. a	6. b	7. a	8. b	9. b	10. c
45	1. b	2. c	3. a	4. a	5. c	6. b	7. a	8. b	9. a	10. a
46	1. b	2. b	3. c	4. a	5. b	6. a	7. c	8. b	9. a	10. b
47	1. c	2. a	3. c	4. b	5. a	6. a	7. c	8. b	9. b	10. c
48	1. b	2. a	3. b	4. a	5. b	6. c	7. a	8. a	9. b	10. b
49	1. b	2. a	3. c	4. c	5. b	6. c	7. c	8. b	9. a	10. a
50	1. a	2. c	3. b	4. b	5. a	6. b	7. a	8. a	9. b	10. a

Progress Graph (1–25)

Directions: Write your comprehension score in the box under the selection number. Then put an x on the line above each box to show your reading time and words-per-minute reading rate.

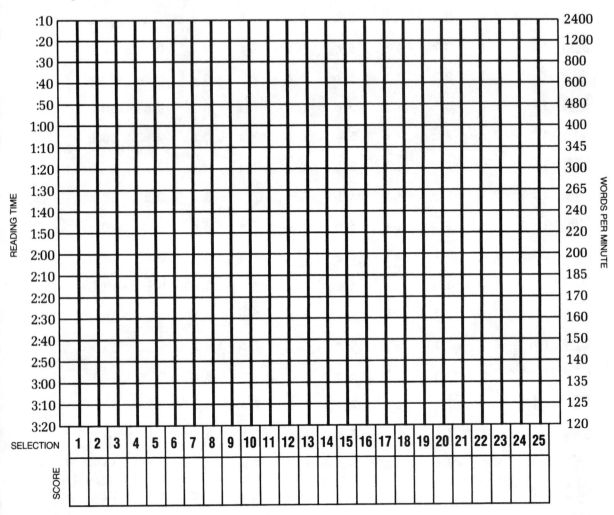

READING TIME		WORDS PER MINUTE
:10		2400
:20		1200
:30		800
:40		600
:50		480
1:00		400
1:10		345
1:20		300
1:30		265
1:40		240
1:50		220
2:00		200
2:10		185
2:20		170
2:30		160
2:40		150
2:50		140
3:00		135
3:10		125
3:20		120

SELECTION: 1 2 3 4 5 6 7 8 9 10 11 12 13 14 15 16 17 18 19 20 21 22 23 24 25

SCORE

Progress Graph (26–50)

Directions: Write your comprehension score in the box under the selection number. Then put an x on the line above each box to show your reading time and words-per-minute reading rate.

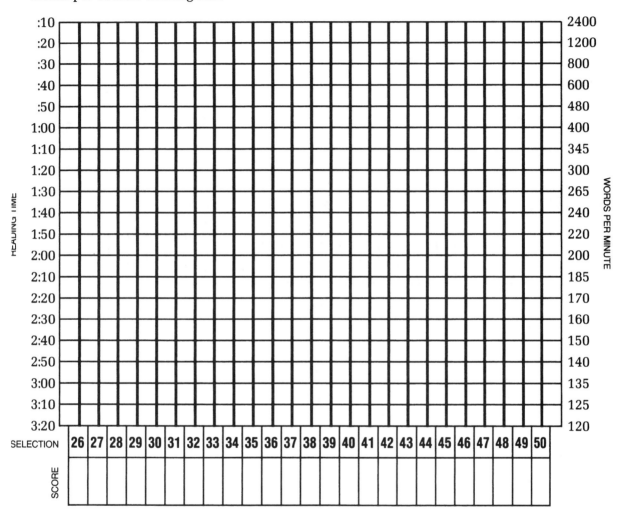

	READING TIME	WORDS PER MINUTE
:10		2400
:20		1200
:30		800
:40		600
:50		480
1:00		400
1:10		345
1:20		300
1:30		265
1:40		240
1:50		220
2:00		200
2:10		185
2:20		170
2:30		160
2:40		150
2:50		140
3:00		135
3:10		125
3:20		120

SELECTION 26 27 28 29 30 31 32 33 34 35 36 37 38 39 40 41 42 43 44 45 46 47 48 49 50

SCORE

Pacing Graph

Directions: In the boxes labeled "Pace" along the bottom of the graph, write your words-per-minute rate. On the vertical line above each box, put an x to indicate your comprehension score.

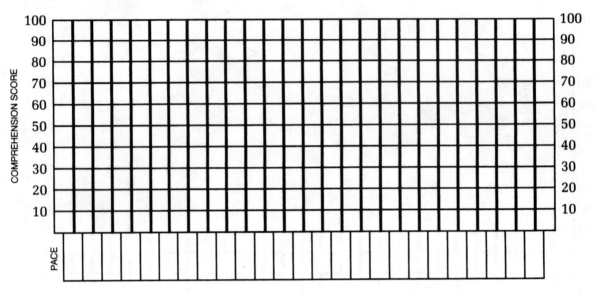